ALSO BY GEORGE HARRISON:

America's Great Outdoors

COAUTHORED WITH KIT HARRISON:

A Beginner's Guide to Birdwatching
America's Favorite Backyard Wildlife
America's Favorite Backyard Birds
Treasury of American Wildlife
Roger Tory Peterson's Dozen Birding Hot Spots

THE BACKYARD BIRD WATCHER *by George H. Harrison*

Technical and Graphic Assistance by KIT HARRISON

A FIRESIDE BOOK
Published by Simon & Schuster
New York London Toronto Sydney Tokyo Singapore

First Fireside Edition, 1988
Published by Simon & Schuster Inc.
Rockefeller Center
1230 Avenue of the Americas
New York, New York 10020
FIRESIDE and colophon are registered trademarks of Simon & Schuster Inc.

Manufactured in the United States of America

10   9
          15   16   17   18   Pbk.

Library of Congress Cataloging in Publication Data

Harrison, George H.
   The backyard bird watcher.

   Bibliography: p.
   Includes index.
   1.   Bird watching.   I.   Title.
QL677.5.H29   598.2'073   78-25956

ISBN 0-671-22664-9
ISBN 0-671-66374-7 Pbk.

The following are authorized reprints:

Chapter 2, pages 49–70. Copyright © 1973, by the National Wildlife Federation. Adapted from "Invite Wildlife to Your Backyard," from the April-May 1973 issue of *National Wildlife.*

Chapter 3, pages 114–17. Feeding station art by Ned Smith. Copyright © 1973 by the National Wildlife Federation. From "How to Make a Holiday Haven for Wildlife," from the December-January 1974 issue of *National Wildlife.*

Chapter 4, pages 166–67. Birdhouse chart. Copyright © 1977 by the National Wildlife Federation. From "Castles in the Air," from the February-March 1977 issue of *National Wildlife.*

Chapter 4, page 169. Bluebird house design. Copyright © 1977 by the National Wildlife Federation. From "Bluebird Homes," from the January 1977 issue of *Ranger Rick's Nature Magazine,* with permission from the January 1976 issue of *The Curious Naturalist.*

Chapter 5, page 187. Pool design, from an undated National Wildlife Federation news release.

Chapter 5, page 190. Dripping bucket art. Copyright © 1974 by the National Wildlife Federation. From "The Finishing Touch Is Water," from the June-July 1974 issue of *National Wildlife.*

Chapter 6, page 200. Squirrel baffle art. Copyright © 1978 by the National Wildlife Federation. From Omnibus page of the April-May 1978 issue of *National Wildlife.*

ACKNOWLEDGMENTS

No book is the product of one person. During the two years that were required to produce this book, many people helped me and I gratefully acknowledge them here:

Kit, my devoted wife, who shared with me every aspect of the production of this work. She is as responsible for the finished product as I. Kit helped with the writing and the photography, and she drew all the backyard diagrams, as well as some of the other line art. She traveled with me every mile, every hour, every word of this effort. She was just as enthusiastic as I about the birds at our feeding station, the loon's appearance each spring, the first sight of the wood duck in our nesting box, the first redwing and the last junco. The use of the "we" throughout the text means Kit and me. Therefore, it is appropriate that this book be dedicated to Kit, for this is not "my" book, but "our" book.

My parents, Mada and Hal Harrison, who encouraged us by sharing their knowledge of the subject, their expertise in the art of writing books and their companionship in the field.

The staff of the National Wildlife Federation, particularly Executive Vice President Tom Kimball, Administrative Vice President Ash Brownridge and Creative Services Director Jim Davis, for sharing information about the Federation's Backyard Wildlife Habitat Program.

John Strohm, Editor of *National* and *International Wildlife* magazines, and Bob Strohm, Managing Editor, for their willingness to allow the use of information from *National Wildlife* that pertains to the sport of backyard bird watching.

Don Hyde, President of Hyde's, Inc., for his help and expertise in the areas of bird feeders and birdhouses, of which Hyde's, Inc., is a major manufacturer.

Sharon and Mike Dunn of Duncraft, Inc., for their help with bird feeders.

F. Robert Scofield of Welles L. Bishop Company, for the use of feeders and birdhouses built by Bishop.

Richard M. Viggars, Pennyfeather Corporation, for sharing a four-year study of bird seed preferences.

Jessie Rapp of Slinger, Wisconsin, and Nancy Andrich of Rubicon, Wisconsin, for conducting bird seed preference studies specifically for this book.

Harald Barry of Vasque Boots, for helping us research appropriate footwear for bird watchers.

Myron Stolp, President of Bushnell, for help in research on binoculars.

Roland Reinders, of Reinders Brothers Seed Company, Elm Grove, Wisconsin, for help in bird seed preference studies.

Betty and Ed Komarek of Thomasville, Georgia, for allowing us to spend several days in their bird room photographing and absorbing the beauties of their spectacular bird view.

Ken Morrison, Mountain Lake Sanctuary, Lake Wales, Florida, for helping us report on that remarkable birding area.

Artist Ralph Winter, Grafton, Wisconsin, for the excellent line art in chapter 2.

Phyllis Ilowite of Milwaukee, who printed nearly every black-and-white photograph.

Ray Quigley of Whittier, California, for excellent darkroom work to convert color photographs into black-and-white.

Richard M. DeGraaf, of the Urban Forestry Research Unit, U.S. Forest Service, Amherst, Massachusetts, for working with us on the technical aspects of backyard habitats, as well as being one of the three readers of the final text before publication.

My sister, Gretchen Gettemy, for reading final text and for making helpful suggestions to improve its readability.

FOR KIT, *whose faith makes the impossible a reality*

Contents

Introduction

BY ROGER TORY PETERSON

How MANY bird watchers are there in the United States? I have often been asked this and can give no clear answer. Estimates (or "guestimates") range all the way from two million to twenty and even forty million, depending on the definition of "bird watcher."

The hard-core "birder" is the person who has seen practically every bird in his *Field Guide* and seldom misses a weekend with his binocular and checklist. Far more numerous are the window-watchers and the garden birders for whom this book has been written. They may not be able to travel to far places for rare and exotic birds but their satisfaction comes from knowing a few familiar species intimately, and hopefully spotting the unexpected visitor that may come through. Over a period of time it is quite possible to tally as many as one hundred species in some suburban gardens. Only a few of these would be resident; many more are seasonal, or simply birds of passage during migration.

There are no endangered species that will be saved by manipulating gardens for wildlife, but there are quite a number of birds whose populations can be built up by such management. The mockingbird is an example. Mockingbirds are basically southern, and although a very few reached New England even in Audubon's time they have become much more numerous in the Northeast during the last twenty years. Because of plantings of berry-bearing shrubs they have become well adapted to suburbia and will even tolerate the bustle of motels and shopping centers.

13

A typical woodlot may average two to three pairs of nesting birds per acre, open country somewhat less, but a suburb with well-managed gardens or a country estate may harbor twice as many. As our cities and towns grow older and more ecologically stable (and not sprayed), more birds will adapt to the contrived environment that they offer. Blue jays are familiar city birds today. They were not in town when I was a boy, fifty or sixty years ago—at least in that part of the country where I lived.

Actually, it is not just for the good of the birds that we attract them to our homes and feed them; it is ultimately for our own pleasure. By sowing our gardens not only with flowers but also with cardinals, orioles, jays, bluebirds, purple finches and goldfinches we are giving ourselves a visual treat and reaffirming the joy and goodness of living. Birds, not rooted to the earth, are among the most eloquent expressions of life.

Winter feeding is more widely practiced than selective planting for birds. In fact, the sale of bird seed mixtures has now become a multimillion-dollar business. Where I live in Connecticut, nearly every house up and down the road has a feeder outside the window.

When I was in my mid-teens over fifty years ago, sunflower seed was only ten cents a pound. Hemp seed cost somewhat less. And as I trudged the two snowy miles to my five feeding stations north of town, I would shuck and chew a few sunflower seeds; they are as addictive as peanuts. I would also pop a handful of hemp seed into my mouth. Recalling this, I suspect that this innocent habit may have been responsible for some of my aberrant behavior when I was a youth. Hemp, I have since learned, is *Cannabis*—marijuana. The birds ate hemp in preference to everything else, and perhaps for good reason. They left the cracked corn and the millet until last. In subsequent years, hemp was "sterilized" before it was sold; later it became unavailable.

Sunflower seed has nearly tripled in price since those early days, and one could go quite broke feeding the flocks of evening grosbeaks that sometimes descend on the feeding tray. At Hawk Mountain in Pennsylvania, Maurice Broun was victimized one winter by several hundreds of these big glamorous finches. He called them "grospigs."

Audubon never saw this attractive species. In his day it was known only from the northwestern part of the continent from Lake Superior to the Rockies. In recent decades the largest offered by tens of thousands if not hundreds of thousands of feeders across the land has extended the winter range of the evening grosbeak eastward to the Atlantic Coast and southward in the Appalachian belt to the Gulf states. Some now remain to nest in New England and the Maritime Provinces.

The cardinal, another big-billed sunflower-seed specialist, has reversed this avian flow. When Audubon stalked the woods it was primarily a bird of the southern states, seldom straying north of New York City. In recent years, because its winter survival has been assured by countless feeders, it has extended its dominion northward to Minnesota, southern Ontario and central New England. The tufted titmouse has followed a similar pattern of range expansion.

Other books have been written about attracting birds, but this one, more imaginatively conceived by George Harrison, avoids being a pedestrian, how-to-do-it book. It is very functional, of course; but it is much more than that. It may even make you a full-fledged "birder" (as distinct from bird watcher), curious about the birds out there that do not come to your garden. One day you might even join one of the special bird-watching tours to Mexico, the Galapagos or East Africa that are becoming so popular. But in the meantime enjoy the robins, the phoebes, the wrens and all the other familiars that give life to the garden. Their return each spring means renewal, confirming the continuity of life.

Foreword

PEOPLE WHO are not aware of birds are missing a kind of sixth sense. Not only do they deny themselves the pleasures of birds, but they are also missing an important and fulfilling link with nature. Birds, like the sun and the rain, the flowers of spring and the colors of autumn, are an amazingly large part of many people's daily existence. Birds tell us that it is morning or that it is evening. They tell us that it is spring or fall. They even tell us that the weather is bad or that it is good. Birds have the capacity to make us feel happy, sad, sympathetic and perplexed. In other words, birds, for many of us, are a manifestation of all nature . . . its beauty, its cruelty, its mystery, its fascination.

I have been aware of birds since I was old enough to notice their movements from my playpen. I have been a serious bird watcher since I was big enough to lift a pair of binoculars to my eyes.

My earliest recollections of birds begin at about the age of three, when my family lived in Tarentum, Pennsylvania, twenty-two miles up the Allegheny River from Pittsburgh. In our backyard, my father built a feeding station for birds consisting of a hanging log with beef suet protruding from the holes, an upside-down old-fashioned wire soap dish to hold more suet against a tree trunk, and several post and hanging seed feeders, including one made from half a coconut shell. These feeders were visited by chickadees, titmice, cardinals, blue jays, nuthatches and woodpeckers. One of my joys as a little boy was helping Dad fill the feeders each winter morning before he went off to work at a local newspaper.

At age 5½ I enjoyed my first backyard feeding station in Tarentum, Pennsylvania, November 1941.

It was a very successful bird feeding station and, in retrospect, I know why. It had all the necessary elements for attracting a wide variety of species: The woodlot behind the house provided excellent cover, the creek meandering through that woods was a source of water that birds require, and the feeding station gave them seed, suet and an occasional tidbit from our table when food in nature was hard to find.

My father did some of his first bird photographs at that feeding station, focusing both his camera as well as my attention on those fascinating birds. I have wondered how much those feeders, and the birds that visited them, influenced both of our careers. It was about that time, during the late 1930s and early 1940s, that Dad decided to become a professional wildlife photographer. His success and my close involvement in it led both of us to pursue vocations in wildlife journalism.

From that time to the present, my family has been consumed by an interest in birds—bird feeding, bird photography, bird study, bird lists, field trips all over the world to see birds, slide programs and later motion picture productions about birds, and many bird books.

At seven, I became a full-fledged bird photographer having successfully recorded on black-and-white film a female catbird feeding

My father, Hal H. Harrison, in the early 1940s when he began his career as an author, photographer and lecturer on birds.

My first bird photograph, taken at age 7, won $10 in a photo contest sponsored by Seventeen magazine.

her young in a neighbor's hedge. That same photograph later won a photo contest conducted by *Seventeen* magazine. At thirteen, I won another photo contest in my hometown which entitled me to a one-year free pass to a local movie theater. The photograph was of a female phoebe sitting on her nest built on top of an electric meter.

And so it went throughout my formative years. Birding and backyard bird watching have not only been part of my life from the beginning, but, as the years have passed, have become the major thrust of my work, my play, my daily existence.

I am not alone. The world is full of people who have rearranged their lives so that they can enjoy the birds they attract to their backyards. Millions have found that bird watching is far more rewarding than most television, theater, sporting events, golf, bridge, sailing, flying, etc. It is also inexpensive, educational and always fresh and different. As I am typing this paragraph, a yellow warbler is bathing in our recirculating pond only a few feet away, a female hairy woodpecker is eating suet at our tree trunk feeder and five goldfinches are busy filling their crops with Niger seed just outside the glass wall in front of me.

A few years ago, when we added a major addition to our home overlooking a small lake in southeastern Wisconsin, Kit and I designed it for maximum bird visibility. On the side of the house where my office and the living room face the lake, we built a floor-to-ceiling wall of Thermopane glass. We did the same upstairs in the master bedroom. Outside these glass walls, we built a patiolike concrete slab bordered by flower boxes and a terrace of wild plants growing under mature trees. In the northeast corner of the patio, a three-tiered, recirculating water pool was constructed for the birds. The so-called patio is more an outdoor studio than anything else. Most of the bird photographs that appear in this book were taken through those Thermopane windows. Nearly all the bird feeding photographs, as well as all those of birds at the pond, were made in this fashion.

The success of this backyard bird habitat, preceded by a lifetime of attending to birds in a series of other backyards through forty years of life, led to the concept of this book.

Before we began working on *The Backyard Bird Watcher*, Kit and I spent more than half the year away from home working on another book. *Roger Tory Peterson's Dozen Birding Hot Spots* required 32,693 miles of travel to those twelve fabulous birding areas. We

My wife Kit and I at our glass wall overlooking the feeding stations where many of the photographs in this book were taken.

had to be at each at the exact time when it was at its peak for bird watching. It was great fun, but, frankly, we missed being home. We missed the many events that occur in any backyard birding habitat ... the first red-winged blackbird of spring; the changing of the male goldfinch's plumage from drab green to bright yellow; the sudden absence of the juncos when they moved north to breed; and their reappearance in the fall to signal winter's approach. Events like these make the bird watcher's year complete, and we missed most of this while searching for bigger game. It occurred to us that there may very well be more birders interested in backyard birding than there are those willing to travel afar to see the more spectacular sights of the bird world. So we decided to spend the next two years at home working on this book. It was most rewarding.

The experiences we have had will live with us forever. They were not spectacular, but they were fulfilling. They were also exasperating, exciting, disappointing, and occasionally heart-rending. But most of all, they were glimpses of life in the outdoors . . . as seen from the windows in the kitchen, the office, the dining room, the bedroom, at the picnic table, and from lawn chairs. We hope that by sharing with you the knowledge we have gained, we can help you become more skilled at attracting birds to your own backyard and more fulfilled by the experiences they bring.

GEORGE H. HARRISON
Hubertus, Wisconsin

1

The Sport of Backyard Bird Watching

WHAT IS a bird watcher? A person who watches birds? I suspect that most people watch birds, and yet many do not consider themselves bird watchers.

The definition of a bird watcher is changing. Thirty years ago, the "typical" bird watcher was exemplified by magazine cartoons as a nattily dressed, elderly person who, from all outward appearances, was eccentric, if not downright odd. That early image of "the little old lady in tennis shoes" gave the sport a stigma which, to this day, makes some people uneasy about admitting that they enjoy watching birds.

Today, the typical bird watcher, or "birder" as we call ourselves, is male, white, married, above average in education and income, and is either retired or a young professional according to one recent study. This may be the *average* bird watcher, but the sport attracts all kinds of people from all walks of life, and their numbers are growing at a dramatic rate.

During a recent telephone conversation with Roger Tory Peterson, the dean of bird watching the world over, I asked him to estimate the number of bird watchers in the United States today. "What is your definition of a bird watcher?" he responded. Before I

A song sparrow eating some of the millions of pounds of bird seed sold in the U.S. each year.

could answer his first question, he went on, "Do you include duck hunters as bird watchers?" We finally settled on the figure of at least twenty million Americans who spend money on bird seed or equipment, or on travel just to see birds.

I believe this is a conservative estimate. A recent study conducted by Richard M. DeGraaf and Brian R. Payne of the U.S. Forest Service Research Unit at the University of Massachusetts in Amherst showed that Americans spend at least $500 million a year to enjoy birds. Of this total, $170 million was spent for bird seed; $187 million for photographic equipment and processing; $115 million for binoculars; $15 million for birdhouses and feeders; and $4 million for bird guides and other books. These figures do not include travel expenditures. Another survey showed that bird watchers and photographers alone accounted for 9,900,600 use-days on National Forest lands in a single year.

So, bird watching may have been the sport of "little old ladies in tennis shoes" at one time, but "you've come a long way, baby" since those days. Bird watching is probably a billion-dollar-a-year industry and may be the fastest growing family sport in America.

Why is it so popular and why is it growing so fast? The answer is simple: The sport of bird watching is easy to get into, inexpensive to maintain, requires little prior knowledge and almost no equipment. Actually, all you need to attract birds to your backyard is a little seed thrown on the ground . . . then wait for the birds in your neighborhood to find it. But if you really want to attract a variety of interesting and colorful birds on a permanent or at least seasonal basis, there are proven ways of doing it, and that's what this book is all about.

LEARN TO IDENTIFY THE BIRDS

Wild birds are everywhere during all seasons, in all habitats. Bird watchers start out by observing the birds they see in their backyards, on their way to work, around their camping areas, etc. Though you certainly don't have to be an expert to enjoy birding, it helps to be able to identify what you see. By being able to recognize the species, you are more likely to learn something about its characteristics and habits.

We identify birds by spotting certain key field marks, behavior, song, size or shape. Thanks to Roger Tory Peterson, who in 1934 wrote and illustrated his first *A Field Guide to the Birds*, we know that every species has its own particular identification signs or marks. Before the Peterson *Field Guide*, bird watching wasn't as much fun. The descriptions of birds were made by scientists who worked largely from study skins in museums. Instead of saying that a robin was a gray-backed bird with a rusty breast, they described it in the minutest detail, including the "white spots around the eye and the streaked throat." Peterson's new system changed the whole

Thanks to Roger Tory Peterson's A Field Guide to the Birds, *first published in 1934, anyone can learn to identify birds by their field marks.*

concept of bird watching by giving us a simple and exact method of quick field identifications.

During my courtship with my wife, Kit, I taught her how to identify birds. Her experience should give encouragement to anyone starting from zero. Within one year, Kit learned to identify over 100 species from sight and sound. The way she did it was to look at each bird she encountered, often through binoculars, listen to it sing or chip, and then check the illustration of that bird in a field guide and read the description of it. I pointed out to her the salient field marks . . . white wing bars, red cap, white outer tail feathers, smaller than a robin, larger than a crow. I would impress upon her the habitat in which it was found, how it was acting, the song or alarm note it gave, and the season of the year in which we found it. She is a quick learner, and within three years she was able to identify 300 to 400 birds and was sometimes correcting my errors in identification. Her pinnacle came two years ago when she and Roger Tory Peterson had a serious discussion comparing the differences between a newly hatched coot chick and a newly hatched chick of the European moorhen.

More recently, Kit and I were amazed to find a birder making accurate field identifications without binoculars. We were in Cuba, birding with that country's foremost ornithologist, Orlando Garrido. While most of us were looking for the field marks through binoculars, Garrido was watching for characteristic movements such as tail bobbing, wing flitting, nervousness, head movement, stance, movement in flights. I tried to catch him in error, but he was always correct and more rapid than I in identifying the bird. He is the most extraordinary field ornithologist I have known.

THE GAMES BACKYARD BIRD WATCHERS PLAY

No matter how you look at it, bird watching is a sport. It is a personal challenge to identify the birds you see, learn their habits and how they differ from other species.

The most common game that bird watchers play is the "listing game." Almost all birders, particularly backyard birders, keep records of the species they see in their neighborhood. Kit and I have recorded 142 species in five years seen through our windows and from our property. Using the official checklist published by the Wisconsin Society for Ornithology, we record, each year, the date on which we see the first bird of each species. This gives us a running record of when the first red-winged blackbird appears each spring, the first junco each fall. The dates vary year to year by as much as two weeks, depending on weather conditions. We also note the date each spring when the ice goes out of our lake, which has a direct effect on the waterfowl we see. We mark the date that the lake freezes over each winter as well.

One of the highlights of our listing game is the appearance of our

The loon that visits our lake stays only a few days, but is living proof that the lake is still wild.

loon each spring. I theorize that any lake that can support a loon, even if for only a few days, is a wild lake. Our lake is located only twenty-six miles northwest of a major metropolitan area. Each spring, our loon spends at least a week with us soon after the ice disappears, and by his appearance declares that our little lake is "wild" for another year. I suspect that there are probably several loons that visit our lake, but we can't differentiate because they all look alike. We did have two at one time several springs ago. Last fall we had a loon headed south in its winter plumage, which was decidedly different from its spring garb. Notes like these are all part of our list.

There are several other kinds of lists, such as the one-day list, which is a record of all the birds seen or heard on a specific day. Some like to keep a trip list or a list of birds seen during a visit to another backyard bird watcher's home. But the most common list is the one that records all those birds seen or heard over a particular year or each of a series of years, like the one we keep.

One backyard birder not only keeps a running list of the birds in her yard but tries to photograph each one as well. She pastes a

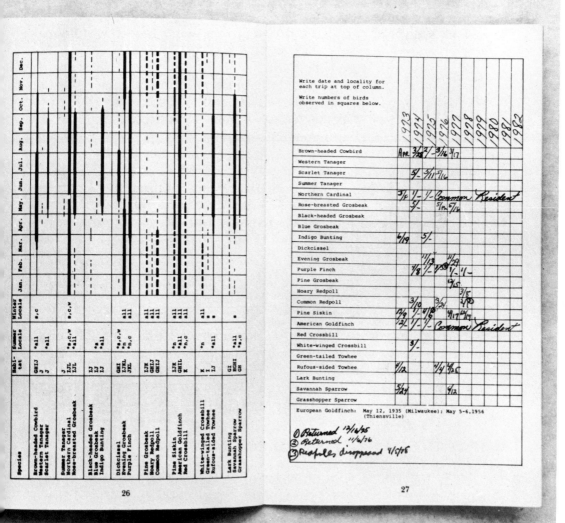

The kind of records I keep on the birds around my backyard reflects the date on which each species is first seen each year.

photographic print on the page of her record book opposite the dates and notes about that particular species. Another backyard birder posts all his records on a large wall chart that is a permanent part of that house's decor. People visiting him can see at a glance the birds he has seen and the dates the sightings were made. It's a great conversation piece.

The most dedicated keep a life list—all those species seen during a lifetime, not just in the backyard, but for North America or for the world. The most radical of those life listers will go to any length to add just one more species to their list. A classic example is the North American champion, Dr. Joseph Taylor of New York. Dr. Taylor had 720 species on his life list when the Ross's gull was sighted in Massachusetts. Dr. Taylor was in Nairobi at the time. Not wanting to miss a rare opportunity to add that species to his North American list, Dr. Taylor flew from Nairobi to Massachusetts, saw the gull and then returned to his African tour. At this writing, Dr. Taylor still leads the life listers with more than 730 North American species.

TELEPHONE LINE FOR BIRDERS

To help listers see more birds, some larger cities have a "birding hot line." It is a telephone number a birder calls to get a taped recording of the current unusual species being seen in the area. The system also enables the caller to give information on an interesting sighting to be added to the tape.

HELP THE CHRISTMAS BIRD COUNT

Each holiday season, during the two weeks centering around Christmas, the National Audubon Society holds its annual Christmas Bird Counts throughout the world. More than 1,200 approved groups of bird watchers count the numbers of species and the numbers of individuals of each species in a fifteen-mile diameter over one twenty-four-hour period during those two weeks. In the U.S., the current record is 216 species, counted in Freeport, Texas. The record for the world was set in the Canal Zone of Panama, where 344 were recorded.

If there is a Christmas bird count in your area and if your backyard falls within the fifteen-mile diameter, offer to help the group by reporting all the species you see on that day in your yard. It is possible that some of the birds you see will not be found anywhere else in the counting area.

Reports on all the Christmas Bird Counts are printed in the National Audubon Society's publication, *American Birds*.

SOME PLAY THE LISTENING GAME

Another game bird watchers play is the "listening" game. The challenge is to be able to identify as many species as possible by the songs or call notes they give. There has always been some disagreement among birders as to the validity of a record of a species that is heard but not seen. Personally, I believe that if you hear the bird and are positive of its song, then you are entitled to record it on your own personal list. However, the American Birding Association, the organization that keeps records of the top U.S. life listers, requires that the bird be seen before it can be officially recorded on a life list. Regardless, the ability to identify a species by its song or alarm note is a great accomplishment. No two species make identical sounds except imitators such as the mockingbird and starling. Once you learn the song of a species, identification is much easier and you don't have to spend time searching out the bird among heavy foliage or at the top of a high conifer.

Warblers are particularly hard to see. When Kit and I are birding in one of our favorite haunts, Mount Desert Island, Maine, the lis-

Kit and I spotted this singing male palm warbler on Mount Desert Island in Maine.

tening game is the only way to go. Blackburnian and bay-breasted warblers are nearly impossible to see in tall spruce trees, but their lovely songs are easy to recognize. If we had to spot each singing male to be sure of its identification, it would take all the fun out of birding in Maine. So the listening game is important and fun to play as you become more adept as a bird watcher.

Some backyard bird watchers record bird songs on tapes, then play them back to get interesting responses, particularly from male birds defending territories in spring and summer.

THE SCIENCE OF BIRD BANDING

A much more specialized game is that of banding birds. In fact, those who band (the British say "ring") don't consider it a game at all, but a serious and scientific effort to learn more about bird movements. Records of bandings and recoveries are kept at the Migratory Bird Research Laboratory, U.S. Fish and Wildlife Service Station, Laurel, Maryland 20811. (See page 230 for what to do when you find a banded bird.)

BREEDING BIRD RECORDS

Another valuable scientific effort is the North American Nest Record Card Program of the Laboratory of Ornithology at Cornell University. Volunteers from all over North America record information about birds' nests they find and send a completed record card to the Cornell Laboratory, where it is fed into computer banks on each species. This information leads to valuable data about population trends and the effects of weather and environmental pollution on certain indicator species. For more information, write The North American Nest Card Program, 150 Sapsucker Woods Road, Ithaca, New York 14853.

THE FLOCKING OF BIRD WATCHERS

The sport of bird watching often leads to social gatherings. When two backyard bird watchers get together for dinner, cocktails, birthdays, other social events or even business meetings, the conversa-

Bird bander Wallace MacBriar untangles a chickadee from the mist net that caught the tiny bird. MacBriar, assistant director of the Milwaukee Museum, has banded more than 30,000 birds since 1937.

Though bird banding is a kind of sport, it is also a serious effort to obtain knowledge about the movements and natural history of birds. This ruby-crowned kinglet was banded and released at the Schlitz Audubon Center, Milwaukee, by bird bander Wally MacBriar.

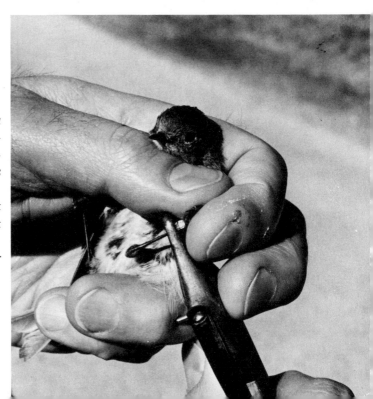

tion inevitably turns to birds. An example of this is our relationship with our good friends, the Tom Rosts, who live in the community of Cedarburg, Wisconsin. Tom is a distinguished wildlife artist, and just outside his studio window is a very active bird feeding station. We see the Rosts about once a month, and a great deal of our visiting time is filled with conversation about the new birds we have seen at each of our homes since our last get-together. Our experience with the Rosts is probably typical of many birders.

Other birding friends join bird clubs to enjoy a more involved kind of ornithological socializing. Foremost among the bird clubs are the local chapters of the National Audubon Society. Most states also have ornithological societies and some have statewide or regional bird clubs as well. (See page 273 for names and addresses of organizations of interest to birders.)

The American Birding Association and the Bird Populations Institute are national associations to which many birders belong. More scientifically oriented birders and professional ornithologists join the American Ornithologists' Union, the Wilson Ornithological Society, the Cooper Ornithological Society or the Cornell Laboratory of Ornithology. The first of these groups, the AOU, concerns itself with, among other endeavors, the taxonomic aspects of ornithology and maintains the official list of both common and scientific names for birds of North America. The AOU has become better known recently for the numerous changes it has made in bird names. For example, there is no longer a Baltimore oriole. It was lumped with the Bullock's oriole and both are now called the northern oriole. The same is true of the myrtle and Audubon warblers. They are now called the yellow-rumped warbler. The AOU made three changes in the name of our common egret, from *American* to *common* to *great*, in the last decade. These changes and many others are based on well-founded scientific study, but some bird watchers get upset, mostly for sentimental reasons, but also because their life lists shrink every time two species are lumped into one.

THE MOBILE BIRD WATCHER

Most enthusiastic backyard bird watchers sooner or later take birding trips. No research has yet been done on how many miles birders travel each year in pursuit of their sport, but it has to be in the many millions. For example, Kit and I traveled 2,500 miles to

No one knows how much money bird watchers spend on travel, but it has to be in the many millions. These Americans went to central Mexico to watch birds recently.

Mexico two years ago just to attend, at that time, the world's top-ranked Christmas Bird Count in Catemaco. We were amazed to find that there were fifty-one other birders there who had also traveled from the United States and Canada to this remote jungle. The attraction was to see nearly 300 different species in a Christmas Bird Count.

We have discovered that one of the pleasures of our travels is our portable bird feeding operation. We carry with us some of our back-yard supplies, which usually include bird seed, anytime we go afield. When we are headed for the Southwest, we also take sugar water and hummingbird feeders. When we stop to camp or for a

These "pot licker" mallards visited our Bear River, Utah, campsite every evening for a handout of bird seed.

picnic lunch, the first chore is to put out bird seed or table scraps on a flat rock nearby. Almost always we attract local populations of birds and mammals. At busy tourist stops, particularly in the West, we often find an eager flock of jays and squirrels ready for a handout.

While producing *Roger Tory Peterson's Dozen Birding Hot Spots*, we fed a pair of mallards at our Bear River, Utah, camp site each evening around suppertime. They ate wild bird seed mixture out of a margarine cup. A few months earlier in Madera Canyon, Arizona, we fed a dozen different species of birds at our camp site, including four kinds of hummingbirds attracted to sugar water.

We find that the same principles that apply to the backyard feeding station at home apply to the portable feeding station on the road. If we select the right kind of habitat for our stops, we have a good chance of having the companionship of local birds for as long as we are there.

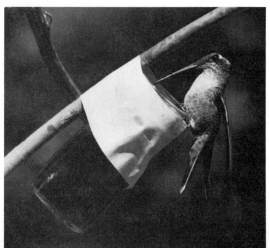

Traveling bird watchers often pack sugar water when they are touring in the West or Southwest, where hummingbirds are common and easily attracted to makeshift feeders like this one in Madera Canyon, Arizona.

THE EARLY BIRDER GETS THE WORM

We have always known that birding is best early in the morning, but we didn't realize how dramatically better it was during early hours until we read the records in the accompanying table, kept by bird bander Wallace MacBriar, who captures birds with a mist net and bands them at the Schlitz Audubon Center in Milwaukee. You can see by this table that after 10:00 A.M. the birds per net-hour drop off dramatically even though the opportunity for capture (mist net-hours) remains relatively high. This indicates that birds are less active during the midday and early afternoon. Note that the number of birds captured between 9 and 10 A.M. is the highest, yet analysis of the opportunity for capture indicates that the period is much less productive than the 6–7 A.M. or the 7–8 A.M. periods.

Hours of Day	Birds Captured	Percent of Total	Mist Net-Hours	Birds/Mist Net-Hour
6–7 A.M.	61	5.3	38.9	1.57
7–8	198	17.2	186.3	1.06
8–9	222	19.3	248.8	0.89
9–10	235	20.4	258.9	0.91
10–11	165	14.3	262.0	0.63
11–12	130	11.3	190.9	0.68
12–1 P.M.	49	4.3	131.5	0.37
1–2	60	5.2	116.5	0.52
2–3	27	2.3	64.9	0.42
3–4	2	0.2	9.6	0.21
4–5	2	0.2	4.2	0.48

A RELATIVELY NEW SPORT

It has only been one hundred years or so since John James Audubon, Henry David Thoreau and, more recently, John Burroughs, wrote about the birds they saw and fed. But the person who may have invented the sport of backyard bird watching in this country was Wells B. Cook, who in 1880 organized people to report on the movements of birds to the U.S. Department of Agriculture. He may have been the first person to challenge Americans to really watch birds. In 1888 Cook published the accumulated information in a report on bird migrations.

Soon afterward, in 1895, Frank M. Chapman wrote *A Handbook of Birds of Eastern North America.* It was a major accomplishment for its time, but compared to modern field guides, it left much to be desired.

The early 1900s produced a host of ornithologists including Edward Howe Forbush, editor of the *Birds of Massachusetts,* Ludlow Griscom and Arthur Allen. The period also produced a number of great American bird artists such as Louis Agassiz Fuertes, Francis Lee Jaques, Allen Brooks, Edmund Sawyer, Bruce Horsfall and, later, Roger Tory Peterson.

But the greatest achievement to date in the field of bird watching is Peterson's *A Field Guide to the Birds,* published in 1934. That one book made bird watching what it is today. It simplified the sport to the point where anyone could learn to enjoy birds. It and its many revisions have remained the bible to this day, and it has made Peterson the high priest of the bird world.

A product of Roger Tory Peterson's "boom in birding," I have watched the sport grow from a handful of dedicated, sometimes abused, people who met quietly in small auditoriums or homes to the national preoccupation that birding has become today. It seems that everyone is watching birds. I know governors, telephone linemen, secretaries, college students, policemen, radio repairmen and space engineers who are all backyard bird watchers. We now find commercial advertising aimed at birders on cereal boxes, in national magazines, on television and in huge department stores. According to *Better Homes and Gardens,* backyard bird feeding has become a kind of winter replacement for gardening. In the summer, backyard birds are, indeed, an integral part of colorful gardens all over America. Recent research by the U.S. Forest Service at the University of Massachusetts in Amherst has given us simple steps that will almost assure the attraction of birds to just about any backyard, and thousands of families are finding that they really work (see chapter 2).

Looking into the crystal ball, I would guess that we have just seen the tip of the iceberg. My instincts say that in another ten years, virtually half the households in America will be feeding birds and that the present billion-dollar-a-year industry will double.

The following pages of this book are designed to give you the knowledge to create your own successful backyard bird habitat, which should lead to more happiness and fulfillment in your life.

Winter feeding stations have become the equivalent of summer gardening in many parts of the U.S.

My children, Peter and Jennie, are already into bird watching. I have told them that regardless of what they do in life, birding can always be an enjoyable part of it.

A FEW ESSENTIAL ITEMS OF EQUIPMENT

Though equipment is not necessary for watching birds in your backyard, these few basic items should help you enjoy birding even more:

• *A Field Guide*—There are a number of good field guides to the birds of North America available in most book stores. The two I like best are *A Field Guide to the Birds*, by Roger Tory Peterson, published by Houghton Mifflin (previously mentioned), and *Birds of North America*, by Robbins, Bruun and Zim, with illustrations by Arthur Singer, published by Golden Press. Both are excellent for beginners as well as experts. Both have color illustrations of each species and descriptive text plus information about range, habitat and other characteristics. They are compact for carrying in the field, and are available in paperback editions. The Peterson book is for eastern species only. His *A Field Guide to Western Birds* covers the balance of the United States and Canada. The newest guide, *The Audubon Society Field Guide to North American Birds* (two volumes), is arranged by bird colors rather than by bird families, which might make identifications easier for beginners but is more difficult for those trained on Peterson guides.

• *Binoculars*—Of the basic equipment needed for total enjoyment of bird watching, a good pair of binoculars is probably the most important. I say "good," because there are many on the market and some are so cheaply manufactured that use of them will actually reduce your enjoyment of birding. Costs run from $50 to $500 a pair.

The three most essential items of equipment needed by bird watchers are sturdy footwear, a good pair of binoculars and a field guide to the birds.

• *How to Buy Binoculars*—Here are some points to consider when buying a pair of binoculars.

Exit pupil test. Hold the binoculars up to the light at about fifteen inches from your eyes. Notice the light coming in through the two eye pieces. If the circle of light comes through in a perfect circular shape, that generally indicates better-grade optics. If the light comes through in a polygon shape, that means you will probably have difficulty in resolving the fine details essential in birding.

Central focus. The style that has one wheel in the middle for focusing both eyes at the same time or the more modern instant-focus lever is called a central focus binocular and achieves fast, sharp focus needed for birding. Central focus models also have a right eye adjustment for eye strength correction, but once that is adjusted for an individual's eye balance, the central wheel adjustment is all that is needed to focus at any distance.

Adjustable cups. Particularly important to people who must wear glasses are adjustable eye cups that screw down (or fold down if made of rubber) to allow your eyeglasses and thus your eyes to get close to the binocular lens. Adjustable eye cups increase the field of vision for wearers of eyeglasses by about 50 percent.

Strength of bridge. The stronger the bridge connecting the two lenses, the fewer problems with alignment.

Heavy construction. The heavier the binocular hinge, the better the assurance of alignment is what the industry tells us, but for bird watchers, weight is a consideration. Some manufacturers do make lighter-weight models of good quality.

Lens coating. Fully coated lenses help limit internal reflection and loss of transmitted light. Front ultraviolet coatings act as haze filters.

Resolution. Select a distant point with fine detail and compare the models you are considering. For the bird watcher, it is important to see the finest details.

Our favorite birding binocular is the Bushnell Custom 7 power × 35mm. This unit is well-built, lightweight, has a wide field of vision, a near-focus of fourteen feet, good resolution, and has screw-down nylon eye cups. Kit and I each have a pair, which are usually sitting on our desks when we are not afield. Kit's office is on the west side of the house, mine on the north. We each have our

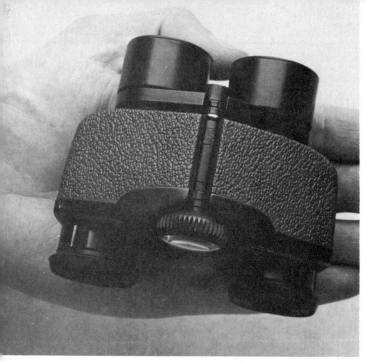

These small and lightweight binoculars made by Bushnell are excellent for taking on business trips.

own "bird window," where binoculars are useful on any given day.

We use another Bushnell binocular for business trips where bird watching may or may not be possible. It is the ultra-lightweight Custom Compact 7 × 26. It is small enough to fit in your pocket, briefcase, or palm of the hand. Though it does not transmit as much light as the Bushnell Custom for serious birding, it is an excellent compromise when packing the larger model is a problem.

• *Binoculars and the Elements*—There are some things to keep in mind when you take your binoculars outside, particularly in the winter.

In very cold weather, don't keep your binoculars too close to your warm body. The contrast of heat and cold causes moisture to condense and fog the lenses.

If you want to keep your binoculars from dangling as you climb a cliff or lean over a mountain stream, put one arm through the strap and carry them across one shoulder and under the other arm. Most binoculars come equipped with long neck straps. Either cut off a few inches or tie a knot in the strap to allow the binoculars to rest on your chest, where they will not sway or bounce as you walk.

For maximum definition of details when outdoors, wear a hat with a bill on the front to shade out the light. When eyes are not shielded, light from the sky causes the pupils to contract, creating a "washed" effect that makes the bird appear dim. When light is

By wearing a hat with a visor and by closing off more light with your hands, maximum visibility can be realized through binoculars.

shielded, the pupil remains large and all the light coming through the binoculars is utilized.

When you are caught in a rain or are birding near saltwater, be sure to wipe your glasses with a damp cloth. Clean the lenses only with lens tissue or a clean linen handkerchief. Blow the grit from the lenses before wiping.

I have discovered that backyard bird watchers sometimes have a problem when using binoculars to see a bird through a kitchen window. If you find that you cannot focus sharply, the problem may be with the glass in the window, not your binoculars. Old or poor quality window glass has imperfections that are magnified through binoculars and camera lenses, causing distortions of your subject. Plate glass, however, is excellent for this purpose, and if your main birding window is not of good quality glass, you might want to replace it. Our glass walls are not only plate glass, but are also Thermopane (two layers), yet we have no problem seeing birds up close through binoculars or camera lenses. We even have success at rather severe angles.

Some birders prefer a spotting scope to binoculars. They like to set up their powerful scopes on a tripod for excellent viewing of birds far beyond the good sighting range of most binoculars. The spotting scope has a definite place in the equipment of the backyard bird watcher. Some of our friends leave their scopes set up in their houses focused on the most popular feeders. When there is some unusual activity or a rare bird appears, they are ready. Not a bad idea. Though we prefer binoculars, we did this last winter when a pair of screech owls moved into our wood duck box. Every morning and evening, the screech owls watched us watch them through a spotting scope.

Equipped with spotting scope, binoculars and field guide carrying case, this Texas bird watcher eyeballs a tropical species in Mexico.

When there is a special birding attraction on my patio, a spotting scope is set up for a closer look. Sometimes it stays in position for weeks.

• *Shoes*—If the backyard bird watcher does all his viewing from inside, there is no need for special footwear. However, most birders we know are inclined to "beat the brush," and shoes are an important consideration for those of us who look for birds in wet, rough and brushy terrain. Tennis shoes are not good for this. Sturdy, leather hiking shoes or boots, costing $30 to $50, are the best. Tough but comfortable footwear will allow you to charge right into thickets without concern for thorns, sharp rocks or nettles.

Kit and I both wear Vasque Explorer boots, an ankle-high, lightweight, rugged hiking shoe with a Vibram sole for good traction and wear. There are many hiking shoes or boots on the market, but most tend to be too heavy for bird watching activities. The Vasque Explorer boots seem to satisfy our needs, and they are very comfortable, fashionable footwear.

• *Backpacks and field guide pouches*—Though certainly not essential, we have found that a simple backpack is a help on most bird walks. We usually carry in it a camera, insect repellent, field guides and sometimes our raincoats. This leaves our hands free to use binoculars or cameras.

Artist friend Ned Smith told us about another way to carry field guides. British army engineer's survey packs, available in army surplus stores, are shaped perfectly for carrying two field guides over the shoulder or on a belt.

A simple backpack or rucksack is a great help in carrying camera, field guide and other things while allowing your hands to be free to use binoculars.

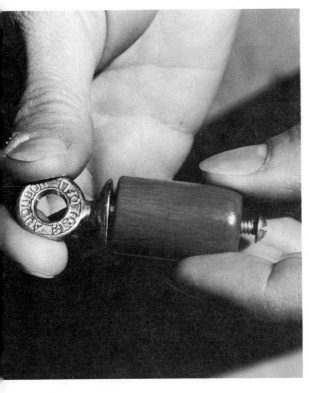

This little device, called an Audubon Bird Call, is great for calling in birds for a closer look.

• *Squeakers*—For a nominal sum, an Audubon Bird Call can be purchased through mail order houses. This little device makes a high-pitched sound that resembles the call of a baby bird and will attract the attention of many species. Some birders "squeak in" birds by merely kissing the back of their hand or the side of the index finger. Regardless of how the noise is made, it is an effective way to get birds in closer for more positive identification.

• *Camera*—The backyard bird watcher has excellent opportunities to produce exciting bird photographs. That subject is treated in detail in chapter 8.

2

Planning and Planting the Backyard Bird Habitat

IT'S SUMMER. Look out your kitchen window. What do you see? A robin is sitting on her nest in the cherry tree. A male oriole is flying across the lawn and up to its hanging basket nest in the ash tree. A female ruby-throated hummingbird is buzzing from one red impatiens to another, sipping nectar as she goes. At the pool, a red-winged blackbird, a female cardinal, two goldfinches and a male rose-breasted grosbeak are drinking and bathing at the same time. Your yard is sweetly scented by blossoms and has a beautiful mixture of natural vegetation and carefully selected cultivated flowers. Your small lawn and garden are well groomed.

The scene changes. It is winter. The ground is white with snow, and the shrubs and evergreens are heavily laden. The yard is alive with hungry birds. The sunflower seed feeders are loaded with evening grosbeaks, cardinals, chickadees, titmice and a pair of nuthatches. The ground feeders are swarming with white-throated, song and tree sparrows and juncos. The Niger seed feeders are filled to capacity with goldfinches, purple finches, redpolls and several pine siskins. On the two big tree trunks, downy, hairy and red-headed woodpeckers compete for the suet. The nuthatches, titmice

A model backyard birding habitat in summer, this Fairport, New York, yard, owned by the Charles Haines family, has all the elements for attracting a great many summer birds.

This Rhinelander, Wisconsin, yard, owned by Roy and Connie Hunter, is an excellent winter birding habitat.

and chickadees alternate between the suet and the seed feeders. You have at least fifty birds in your yard at this moment . . . don't you?

I have *not* described your yard? You do *not* have all those birds? Well, why not? You certainly could.

Take another look. What is growing there? Do you have a subdivision yard with a large lawn and few, if any, trees and shrubs? That may be why you don't have many birds, even with the feeders.

All birds—indeed, all wildlife—have three basic requirements for survival: cover, food and water. If you provide these three essentials in your backyard, you, too, can have the kind of bird-life bonanza described in the first few paragraphs. The Amherst formula will simplify it for you.

THE AMHERST FORMULA

In the early 1970s, a research team working at the Urban Forestry Research Unit of the U.S. Forest Service at the University of Massachusetts in Amherst, studied the habitat needs of wildlife living in an urban environment. In 1973, as managing editor of *National Wildlife* magazine, I worked with that team to produce one of the most significant articles ever published in *National Wildlife*. Jack Ward Thomas, then project leader at Amherst; Richard M. DeGraaf, wildlife biologist; and Robert O. Brush, a landscape architect, agreed to write the article. "Invite Wildlife to your Backyard" spelled out simple step-by-step plans for enhancing wildlife habitat, primarily by providing cover and food-bearing plants, in the average American backyard. Milwaukee artist Ralph Winter illustrated the successful article, which was reprinted and distributed to over three million people. Thousands of *National Wildlife* readers followed the recommendations and converted their yards into miniature wildlife refuges.

A year later, the National Wildlife Federation began its "National Wildlife Backyard Habitat" program, which certifies any backyard that has successfully attracted a significant amount of wildlife through the development of natural habitat (food, cover and water).

The following describes the Amherst formula, which, if followed, is almost guaranteed to attract birds to any backyard, no matter how large or small.

THE NATIONAL WILDLIFE FEDERATION says:

Invite wildlife to your backyard

BY JACK WARD THOMAS, ROBERT O. BRUSH AND RICHARD M. DeGRAAF

GO OUT IN YOUR BACKYARD and look around. Watch the fish weaving among the water lilies, the dragonflies moving in glittering arcs above the little pool. Don't move — the robins are busy feeding their youngsters in that nest above your head; squirrels are edging down the beech

Your backyard can look like this — for as little as $200 and a plan like ours. This lot, viewed from the rear, has the mature plantings that attract a maximum variety of wildlife. On page 7, you can see this idealized wildlife habitat as viewed from the house patio.

trunks behind you and darting into the shrubbery. The wisteria on your stone wall is almost irresistible to the hummingbird that just appeared, and song sparrows are adding their notes to a tangle of birdsong sifting down from the oaks and maples. If you're really patient, that timid cottontail might bring her brood onto the grass for one last taste of the dew-silvered grass.

This isn't your yard, you say? It could be. If you have even a quarter-acre of crabgrass right now, you can turn it into a wildlife habitat as beautiful and gratifying as the one above. A few square yards — yes, even a window box

Reprinted from April-May National Wildlife Magazine A membership publication of the National Wildlife Federation 1412 16th St. N.W. Washington, D.C. 20036

The National Wildlife *magazine article that launched the National Wildlife Federation's Backyard Wildlife Habitat Program was published first in the April/May 1973 issue. Since then, thousands of Americans have converted their backyards into wildlife refuges.*

MAKE A PLAN

First, you need a plan. No matter how crudely done, you need to sketch out the borders of your yard. Identify what is planted or built into it now, and what you want to plant and build into it in the future. Even if nothing but grass grows there now, you can design and build a model backyard habitat for birds. But take your time. The first simple sketch could determine the whole course of your backyard habitat over the next forty years.

COVER AND REPRODUCTIVE AREAS

All birds need places where they are protected from predators and weather, places where they feel safe to hide, to rest and to raise their young. These places are called "cover." Most natural cover consists of trees, shrubs and plants. Ideally, the same vegetation will also provide "reproduction areas" *and* food in the form of berries, seeds, buds and nuts. An intelligent selection of cover plants is

Cover can be provided in many forms. This fence row is heavily planted with food- and cover-producing shrubs that are ideal for birds.

Cover also means reproductive areas, those places where birds like this mourning dove and other wildlife can find protection and seclusion for nesting and raising young.

the foundation of any model backyard bird habitat. The Amherst list of suggested plants is on page 66.

In addition to plantings, most people allow corners of their yard to grow wild. A family in Fort Morgan, Colorado, let the weeds (which are really flowering plants) grow in one part of their yard to produce both food and cover for their birds the year around. "After adding an addition and patio to our house," they explained, "we let the terrace between the patio and the lake grow wild. Now it is filled with seed-producing weeds and excellent cover. It also has many places for birds to hide and nest," they added.

In Watertown, Wisconsin, a backyard birder turned a formal garden into a bed of weeds by allowing it to grow wild. The weeds grew seeds that fed his birds through the winter. A feeding station provided auxiliary food.

Rock walls or rock piles provide cover for wrens and other wildlife.

Brush piles offer good cover for all ground-feeding birds, such as sparrows, towhees, juncos, winter wrens, thrushes and some ground-inhabiting warblers.

REGIONAL EQUIVALENTS FOR PLANTINGS

The plant materials listed on pages 66 grow best in the Northeast. Use this list to select those best suited to other areas.

Region	Herbaceous Growth	Low Shrubs	Tall Shrubs	Small Trees	Tall Trees
NORTHEAST	Panicgrass, Timothy, Sunflower	Blackberry, Blueberry, Huckleberry, Snowberry	Sumac, Dogwood, Elderberry, Winterberry, Autumn olive, Wisteria	Flowering dogwood, Crab apple, Hawthorn, Cherry, Serviceberry, Red cedar	*Coniferous:* White pine, Hemlock, Colorado spruce; *Deciduous:* Sugar maple, White oak, Red oak, Beech, Birch
SOUTHEAST	*Lespedeya* spp., Panicgrass, Sunflower	Blackberry, Blueberry, Bayberry, Spicebush, Huckleberry	Sumac, Dogwood, Elderberry	Holly, Dogwood, Serviceberry, Cherry, Persimmon, Red cedar, Palmetto, Hawthorn, Crab apple	*Coniferous:* Longleaf pine, Loblolly pine, Shortleaf pine; *Deciduous:* Ash, Beech, Walnut, Live oak, Southern red oak, Black gum, Pecan, Hackberry
NORTHWEST	Turkey-mullein, Timothy, Sunflower, Filaree, Lupine, Fiddlenecks, Tarweed	Blackberry, Blueberry, Snowberry, Oregon grape	Sumac, Bitterbrush, Russian olive, Elderberry, Buckthorn, Madrone	Serviceberry, Dogwood, Hawthorn	*Coniferous:* Douglas fir, Ponderosa pine, Western white pine, Lodgepole pine, Colorado spruce; *Deciduous:* Oregon white oak, California black oak, Bigleaf maple
SOUTHWEST	Turkey-mullein, Sunflower, Filaree, Lupine, Fiddlenecks	Utah juniper, Blackberry, Spicebush, Prickly pear, Algerita	Mulberry, Lote bush, Sumac, Manzanita, Madrone	Serviceberry, Dogwood, Mesquite, Crab apple	*Coniferous:* Arizona cypress, Pinon pine; *Deciduous:* Live oak, Pine oak, Bitter cherry

If you are lucky enough to live on a lake or pond, consider planting food and cover at the water's edge. A bird watcher in Contonment, Florida, planted pecans, magnolias, live oak, pines, dogwoods, crepe myrtle and orange trees along his shoreline. His birds love it.

More reports of birding success directly attributed to cover and reproductive areas include a Wisconsin family who had a mourning dove nesting regularly in their apple tree and cliff swallows under the roof of their shed; an Iowa family who, surprisingly, had three pairs of nesting wrens in the same yard; a Pennsylvania family who had a brood of pheasants raised in their yard; a Virginia family who enticed a pair of bluebirds into their subdivision; and an Indiana backyard habitat that reported a wood duck pair which raised young.

Don't throw away the family Christmas tree. Tie it to a fence post or the trunk of a taller tree, where it will give excellent bird cover for at least a year.

Ideal cover plants also grow food for birds. A cedar waxwing partakes of bittersweet berries, an example of a dual-purpose cover plant.

FOOD

There are many reasons why birds frequent a backyard wildlife habitat, but I believe the presence of food combined with cover is the most common. If a backyard offers nothing but food, it may still attract a limited number of birds on a fairly regular basis, but the combination of food and cover is better.

The easiest way to feed birds is by setting out wild bird seed, suet and various kinds of nuts and fruits. The next chapter, on bird feeding, will deal with this subject in detail.

Nandina produces excellent cover as well as bright orange berries that are relished by mockingbirds, catbirds, robins and others in a Thomasville, Georgia, backyard.

Far more practical and less expensive than buying bird food is planting food-bearing trees, shrubs and plants in your backyard, such as those suggested by the Amherst formula on page 66. If you live in a semitropical or desert region, then plant desert or tropical equivalents of those on the list, such as cactus and pyracantha to produce the fruits and berries that birds in those habitats love. Mesquite and acacia grow bean pods. Oleander and agave flowers produce nectars that are favorites among desert orioles and hummingbirds.

Another good way to provide natural food is to sow seed-bearing plants in your vegetable garden. These would include sunflowers, lespedeza, millet, milo, corn and oats. Plan to leave these plants standing all winter for the birds.

American holly makes a lovely decorative tree and also provides good cover and food for a variety of bird species. This holly was growing in an Easton, Pennsylvania, backyard habitat.

Mountain ash berries, growing in the backyard habitat of the Robert Vanderpoel family of Des Plaines, Illinois, make excellent fall and winter food for a number of species.

A sure way to attract hummingbirds to a backyard is to plant trumpet vine. They also like impatiens flowers.

Bird feeders supplement natural foods in a well-planned backyard birding habitat.

WATER

Without water, the songbirds in your backyard cannot survive. Therefore it should be a part of every plan for a backyard habitat. Water is treated in detail in chapter 5.

HOW MUCH WILL IT COST?

The cost is up to you. If you have a big backyard and want to hire a professional landscaper to do all the work for you, the cost will be high. On the other hand, you can do it for very little by making your own plans and providing your own labor. If you elect to do it yourself, go on a scavenger hunt for free plant materials from Uncle Frank's farm (be sure that Uncle Frank approves of your removing the plants).

Keep in mind, however, that the more of this work you have done professionally, the faster the results and the better the survival rate of the transplanted vegetation. On the other hand, if you do it all yourself, you will derive much more satisfaction from having created this beautiful and productive habitat with your own hands.

These expenditures do not include maintenance, but the average maintenance cost for a well-designed backyard habitat is about the same as it is for the fertilizer, water and labor needed to maintain a well-groomed lawn.

Building a model habitat for birds can cost as little as $200 if you provide your own muscle power and obtain plant materials from Uncle Frank's farm.

HOW BIG A YARD? HOW SMALL?

The Amherst study showed that the average suburban backyard in America is about 100 feet by 120 feet (about a quarter of an acre). If your backyard is smaller, it may be difficult to provide all the items they suggest, and therefore you may want to cooperate with a neighbor. Even people who live in an apartment can successfully attract birds to window boxes by providing a microcosm of the backyard habitat—offering cover, food and water.

If your yard is larger than 100 by 120 feet, you can use the same basic plan to create a backyard habitat that should be more effective because your habitat will be more plentiful, diverse and stable.

WHEN DO YOU START?

Start right now, regardless of the season. If it is not early spring, which is the best time to plant cover, then perfect your all-important plan, clear out plants of no wildlife value and prepare your soil for later planting. If it is winter, make your plan and then build bird feeders, bird boxes and robin shelters. Design a water system if you want to have something more than a standard bird bath.

STAGE I

If you start with nothing but a lawn, then plant the trees, shrubs and herbs suggested in the drawing based on the Amherst design on page 64 and in the chart on page 66. If you can complete all this in the first spring, you will already be at Stage I. As you plant your yard, keep in mind the eventual heights and widths of your trees. These basic plantings, though small, will provide some immediate, though sparse, cover and some natural food for winter. To provide additional cover, build brush piles, place last year's dead Christmas tree upright in a sparse corner, and don't be in a hurry to weed around the pond and shrubs. For breeding places, put up birdhouses and shelters (see chapter 4). To supplement the pond, a bird bath in another part of the yard will help (see chapter 5). Set out feeders to get birds through the first few winters while the natural food is maturing. Even then, you probably will want to maintain feeders every winter even after the vegetation in your yard has matured (see chapter 3).

Stage I: First-year planting
shrubs low
trees scattered

STAGE II

If you start from scratch, it will take five to ten years before your yard reaches Stage II. Many people start with some mature trees and shrubs already growing and, with some thinning and planting, they may be to Stage II the first year. Stage II is very rewarding. In some ways, it will be as successful as the final and mature stage because

Stage II: 5–10-year growth
   shrubs almost full size
   trees 25 feet high

the vegetation is producing maximum yields of food and cover. There will be enough flowers and fruits to attract a great variety of field and woodland birds. Robins, cardinals, chipping sparrows and catbirds will nest in the shrubs and small trees, song sparrows and towhees will find nesting sites in the dense ground cover. The pond will attract regular visitors all day, all night, all summer, and even through the winter if it is heated.

KEY TO BACKYARD PLANTINGS

This list contains the plant materials suggested in a backyard wildlife plan for the Northeast. You may substitute others (see list on page 56), but remember to select a variety of species that produce a year-round supply of food. Also, be sure that moisture and light requirements match your yard's conditions.

All the plants are available at commercial nurseries; many can also be transplanted from the wild.

Species	Mature Height	Flowers	Fruits	Sun/Shade	Wet/Dry	Wildlife Served
TREES						
1. Beech	50–100'		Sept-Oct	Lt shd/sun	Moist	Nuts, seeds, acorns: fall and winter food for squirrels, large songbirds.
2. Red oak	50–100'		Sept-Oct	Lt shd/sun	Moist	Spring, summer foliage: cover and reproductive areas for songbirds, tree-dwelling mammals, insects.
3. White oak	40–100'		Sept-Nov	Lt shd/sun	Moist/dry	Leafless branches: winter roosting for birds.
4. Red maple	40–100'			Shd/sun	Moist/ well-drained	
5. White pine	40–100'		Aug-Sept	Sun	Dry	Cones: fall, winter food for pine squirrels, songbirds. Boughs: year-round cover, reproductive areas for songbirds, tree-dwelling mammals, insects.
6. White spruce	40–100'		Aug-Sept	Sun	Dry	
7. Hemlock	50–80'			Shd/sun	Moist	
8. Red cedar	30–80'		Sept-May	Sun	Moist/dry	
SMALL TREES						
9. Winterberry	10'	May	Oct	Lt shd	Wet/moist	Flowers: food for butterflies, other insects. Berries, fruit: fall, winter
10. Flowering dogwood	10–40'	Mar-June	Aug-Nov	Sun	Well-drained/ dry	

SHRUBS

#	Name	Height	Bloom	Fruit	Light	Moisture
11.	Hawthorn	10–20'	June	Oct–Mar	Sun	Dry
12.	Crab apple	15–30'	Mar–May	Sept–Nov	Sun	Moist/dry
13.	Autumn olive	10'	May–July	Sept–Feb	Sun/lt shd	Moist/dry
14.	Silky dogwood	6–8'	May–July	Aug–Sept	Sun/lt shd	Wet to dry
15.	Red osier dogwood	to 10'	May–Aug	July–Oct	Sun	Moist/wet
16.	Elderberry	3–13'	June–July	Aug–Sept	Sun	Moist/wet
17.	Blackberry	to 10'	May–July	July–Sept	Sun	Moist
18.	Rhododendron	10–15'	May–July	Aug–Dec	Shd	Moist
19.	Honeysuckle	to 10'	June–July	July–Sept	Sun/shd	Well-drained/dry

food for songbirds. Spring, summer foliage: cover, reproductive areas for songbirds. Leafless branches: winter cover, roosting for songbirds.

Spring, early summer flowers: food for butterflies, other insects. Berries: food for songbirds. Foliage: cover, reproductive areas for songbirds, mammals, reptiles, amphibians, insects. Dead branches: winter cover for ground-dwelling mammals and birds.

Spring flowers: food for butterflies, other insects, hummingbirds. Foliage: dense cover, reproductive areas for songbirds, mammals. Rhododendron foliage: winter cover for songbirds, mammals.

ANNUAL FLOWERS

#	Name	Height	Bloom	Fruit	Light	Moisture
20.	Sunflowers	to 5'	Aug–Oct	Sept–Nov	Sun	Moist/dry
21.	Asters	to 4'	Aug–Oct	Sept–Nov	Sun	Moist
22.	Daisies	to 2'	June–Aug	July–Sept	Sun	Dry
23.	Marigolds	to 2'	Aug–Oct	Sept–Nov	Sun	Moist/dry
24.	Black-eyed Susans	to 2'	June–Sept	July–Sept	Sun	Dry

Flowers: food for butterflies, other insects. Seeds: late-summer, fall, winter food for many seed-eating birds, especially sparrows.

STAGE III

It will take thirty to forty years after the initial plantings, if you have started from scratch, to obtain a yard with mature trees and shrubs. Many people already have mature trees when they build their habitats and merely have to plant shrubs and flowers to achieve Stage III the first year.

One of the problems with Stage III is keeping foliage pruned and open enough to attract maximum numbers of birds. Most birds do not like a mature woodland with no ground cover. You must keep some parts of the habitat open to allow sunlight to promote continuous new growth.

Stage III: 30–40-year growth
mature trees
massed clumps of vegetation

If all goes well, Stage III is the ultimate and will attract the greatest number of species for the longest periods of the year. There will be tanagers, orioles and rose-breasted grosbeaks in the summer; hairy woodpeckers, evening grosbeaks, redpolls and crossbills in the winter. During spring and fall migration, the cover, food and water will act as a magnet for birds passing through the area. Many will spend days feeding and resting before making the next journey north or south.

At night, you may have owls and perhaps even a whippoorwill calling. In the early morning you may be awakened by the songs of thrushes and wood pewees.

IS IT WORTH IT?

Beyond the aesthetic values described above, there are other, more practical considerations for going to all the trouble to build a backyard habitat for birds. Real estate people say that the development of such a habitat can increase property values by three to ten percent. In other words, the time and money invested can bring a good monetary return in addition to the pleasure and pride you derive from having a beautiful yard full of birds.

MORE HELP

For additional help, go to your lawn and garden center or local nurseryman. Even if you don't hire him to do the work, he will have some good advice for you. Many of the ornamental plants at the better garden centers are now labeled as "good for attracting birds."

Other sources are your county agent, college extension service or any university landscape specialist. If you live in a soil conservation district, you can get help from that office on water and soil matters. The state office of the Soil Conservation Service has a wildlife biologist who can help. Even big city zoos and museums will be helpful.

Write to the National Wildlife Federation for their free reprint, "Invite Wildlife to Your Backyard," at 1412 Sixteenth Street N.W., Washington, D.C. 20036. When you are ready to register your backyard in the National Wildlife Backyard Habitat Program, write for information from the same address.

HOW SUCCESSFUL ARE THE BACKYARD WILDLIFE HABITATS?

To find out just how successful backyard wildlife habitats have been, the National Wildlife Federation contacted 255 certified backyard owners in forty states and asked them questions relating to their efforts. The survey showed that an average of nineteen new trees and twenty-three shrubs were planted in their yards; five to six bird feeders were erected; nearly everyone provided a source of water; many heated water in winter to keep it ice-free; the average

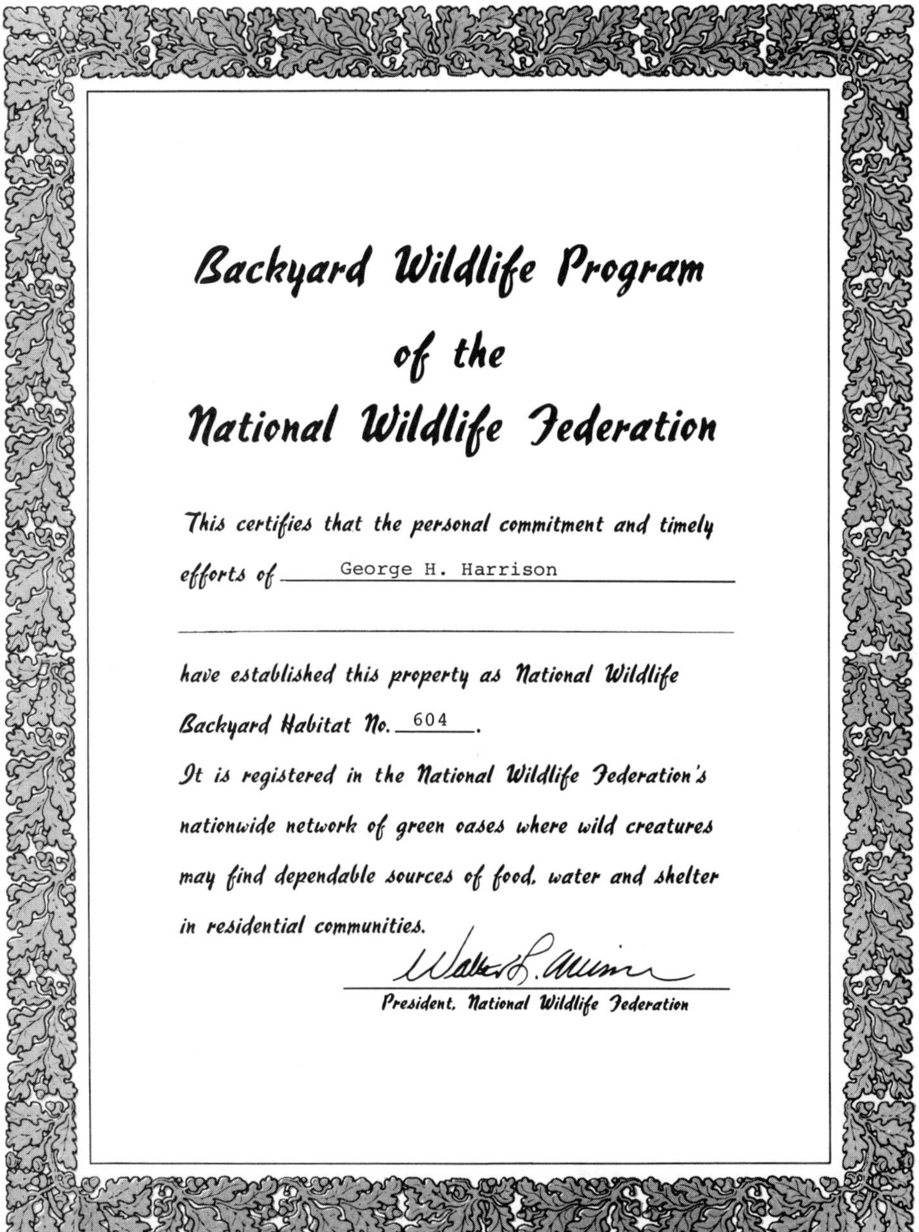

Backyard Wildlife Program

of the

National Wildlife Federation

This certifies that the personal commitment and timely

efforts of _____George H. Harrison_____

_____

have established this property as National Wildlife

Backyard Habitat No. __604__ .

It is registered in the National Wildlife Federation's

nationwide network of green oases where wild creatures

may find dependable sources of food, water and shelter

in residential communities.

President, National Wildlife Federation

Each qualifying backyard in the National Wildlife Federation's Backyard Wildlife Program receives a certificate. My yard is number 604.

expenditures ran about $450, though that figure was inflated by two families who spent $10,000 each to make their backyards more attractive to wildlife.

The investments appear to have paid off. Over ninety percent of the homeowners reported a substantial increase in wildlife activity on their property. In addition, virtually everyone surveyed has convinced a neighbor to develop a habitat.

"It's interesting to speculate about the effects of this increased feeding on wild bird populations," Dick DeGraaf of the U.S. Forest Service at Amherst told me. He went on to say that for a variety of reasons as many as ten new species have appeared in the Northeast. "Winter feeding," he added, "has allowed some southern species, such as cardinals, tufted titmice and mockingbirds, to survive the severe weather."

Rock walls, thick shrubbery and water are the perfect combination for bringing in the birds at the Amherst, Massachusetts, home of wildlife biologist Dick DeGraaf.

MODEL BACKYARD HABITATS

Kit and I wanted to see for ourselves how successful these efforts were, so we visited dozens of backyards around America interviewing the owners and photographing their efforts. The following ten were among the best. Most of these are certified in the National Wildlife Federation's Backyard Habitat Program.

• *St. John's, Michigan:* When Walter and Barbara Steward bought their home in 1970, the entire area had been bulldozed. Every tree, bush and shrub had been scraped off to prepare for their subdivision.

Having moved from a farm they had been renting, the Stewards missed the woods, fields and wildlife they had grown to enjoy in the country. Their new yard was a mudhole . . . and they saw no wildlife.

By their second year, they were ready to do something about their backyard, and when they read the *National Wildlife* article in 1973, they launched their own backyard habitat program. Their first and most expensive effort was to have their mudhole filled. That cost $300. Their total expenses after that were only about $50.

With much love and hard work they planted food and cover in the form of mulberry trees, Russian olives, oaks, a chokecherry, Chinese chestnuts, hickory, evergreens, crab apples, sumacs and one American holly. Spaced around the trees they planted honeysuckle, grape, dogwood, barberry, huckleberry, sunflowers, trumpet vines, spicebush, snowberry and Virginia creeper.

After establishing the food and cover plants, they set up a feeding station with seed and suet feeders.

Water was their next problem. To solve that, they dug a shallow hole, lined it with plastic and created a 3 × 4 foot pool that they kept filled using a garden hose. They also installed an ordinary bird bath in another corner of the yard.

The final consideration was to create reproductive areas. Old Christmas trees started a brush pile near the garden, keeping sparrows and other ground inhabitants happy. Birdhouses were hung to attract wrens. The large trees offered other nesting possibilities.

The yard was finished by surrounding it with a board fence to keep out dogs. Wood for the fence came from an old barn in exchange for the labor to dismantle the structure.

For the next several summers, the Stewards did not take their usual vacation trip "up North." They worked twelve to fifteen hours a week on their backyard and relaxed in it during leisure

STEWARD YARD, ST. JOHN'S, MICHIGAN

 1. Cedar
 2. Maple
 3. Mulberry
 4. Wild roses
 5. Assorted pine and
    spruce
 6. Red osier dogwood
 7. Russian olive
 8. Snowberry
 9. Box elder
10. Apricot tree
11. Gray birch
12. Oregon grape
13. Forsythia
14. Japanese quince
15. Weeping willow
16. Crab apple
17. Spreading juniper
18. Barberry
19. Pussy willow
20. Bush honeysuckle
21. Weeping willow
22. Cottonwood
23. Mock orange
24. Mugho pine
25. Euonymus
26. Flowering almond
27. Spice bush
28. Hybrid elm
29. Nesting spruce
30. Rose of Sharon
31. Grapes

A. Birdhouse or nesting
   shelf
B. Rock pile (under wild
   roses)
C. Brush pile
D. Bird feeder
E. Pool
F. Bird bath

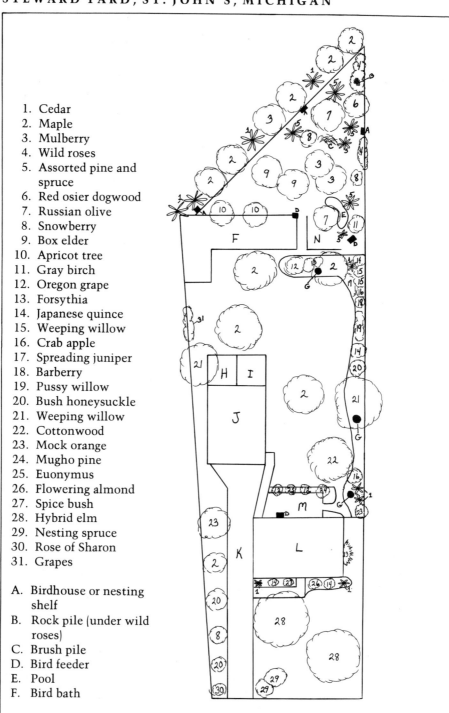

Walter and Barbara Steward of St. John's, Michigan, built one of the first qualifying backyards in the National Wildlife Federation's program. From mud hole to a model habitat, the Stewards' yard had reached Stage I in a little over a year.

Among the many habitat improvements, the Stewards built brush piles for ground-inhabiting birds and mammals.

hours. The results were dramatic. Starting from nothing, they have attracted some twenty different kinds of birds, a half dozen mammals, toads, butterflies, and many insects including a swarm of wild honey bees which they have hived and from which they are harvesting honey.

Was it all worth it? You bet it was. Their yard and their wildlife have become the central focus of their lives. They appear to be very contented people.

• *West Hartford, Connecticut:* In the early 1970s, nothing but grass grew under the mature trees in the backyard of Dr. and Mrs. Edmund Thorne. There was no wildlife there.

THORNE YARD, WEST HARTFORD, CONNECTICUT

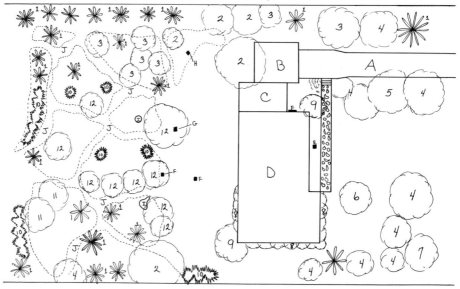

1. White pine	A. Driveway
2. Oak	B. Garage
3. Birch	C. Porch
4. Flowering dogwood	D. House
5. Weeping cherry	E. Niger seed feeder
6. Flowering crab	F. Sunflower seed feeder
7. Japanese maple	G. Suet feeder
8. Shrubs	H. Wren house
9. Amalanchier	I. Water
10. Hemlocks	J. Path
11. Maple	
12. Hickory	

Dot and Edmund Thorne of West Hartford, Connecticut, started out to create a wildflower garden in their backyard, but in the process developed an ideal bird sanctuary.

Then, an interest in photographing wildflowers caused the retired superintendent of West Hartford schools and his wife, Dot, to establish a wildflower garden in their backyard. The idea was "to bring the flowers closer to my lens," chuckled Dr. Thorne. "Planting wildflowers in my backyard has permitted me to photograph them when the blooms are just right."

In place of grass, the Thornes mulched the soil with leaves and pine needles and then began to plant small trees, now numbering seventy laurels, twelve blueberries, thirteen rhododendrons, nine dogwoods and others. Around the trees and shrubs, they planted seventy-five species of wildflowers. In their efforts to establish a wildflower garden, they had created a perfect wildlife habitat—all the ingredients for an ideal bird sanctuary. Food was provided artificially with feeders as well as naturally from food-bearing trees, shrubs and flowers. Cover and reproductive areas were abundant in the vegetation, brush piles and nesting boxes. Birds could drink and bathe in a conventional bird bath that was filled daily. (The Thornes have plans to install a recirculating waterfall as soon as their favorite contractor is available.)

Its close proximity to a natural pond and woodland made the Thorne yard more immediately attractive to wildlife, and it wasn't long before there were more than flowers living in the Thorne habitat. Edmund found his lens being pointed at many kinds of birds as well as raccoons, chipmunks, squirrels, toads, and even a painted turtle looking for a place to lay its eggs. One day a mallard hen and her ducklings from a nearby pond came waddling into the Thorne yard. A female cottontail made a nest under one of the shrubs. The yard was alive with wildlife!

Visitors to date were twenty-two different kinds of birds, five mammals, including an unwelcome woodchuck, several reptiles and amphibians, many butterflies and colorful insects.

An unappreciative neighbor trapped squirrels and released them in the country, which did not particularly please the Thornes. Other than that, the neighbors have joined in the spirit of the habitat. Another neighbor allowed Dr. Thorne to transplant one of the "weeds" from her yard into his. She was later amazed to find that her weed was blooming beautifully.

• *Easton, Pennsylvania:* Faced with their own habitat crisis in a big city, Fred and Carol Mebus turned to the natural world and wildlife for insulation from encroaching humans.

When they bought their hundred-year-old farmhouse, they were surrounded by fields and woodlands. They were out with the wildlife where they wanted to be. But all that ended when the farmer from whom they purchased their land subdivided the surrounding fields and started selling lots. Quickly the Mebuses scraped together enough money to buy an additional 3 acres, giving them about 4½ acres of natural land for a buffer.

Houses were going up all around them, and they felt they needed to do even more to safeguard their island of natural habitat. The gift of a bird feeder started their interest in bird watching, which eventually led to the redesigning of their yard into a model wildlife habitat.

First, they let most of the tract grow wild. This meant that pokeberry and other food-bearing weeds were left to grow and produce.

MEBUS YARD, EASTON, PENNSYLVANIA

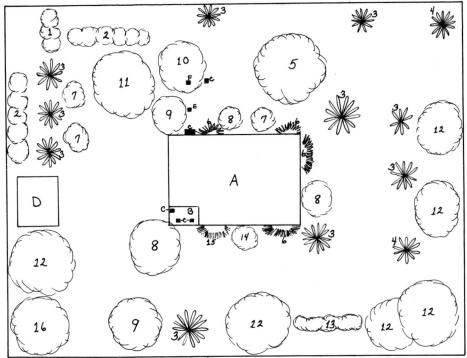

1. Highbush cranberry
2. Lilacs
3. Spruce
4. Pine
5. White birch
6. Yews
7. American holly
8. Dogwood
9. Crab apple
10. English walnut
11. Willow
12. Maple
13. Barberry
14. Pyracantha
15. Juniper
16. Box elder

A. House
B. Porch
C. Bird feeder
D. Shed
E. Niger seed feeder
F. Suet

Their original property already had many mature trees and shrubs plus a great deal of understory. On the new property they planted nine maples, four box elders, five white pines, five blue spruce, two English walnuts and a great many shrubs, including fifteen multiflora roses.

Natural food produced on the property was supplemented with bird feeder food, and for night visitors, the Mebuses put table scraps

When Fred and Carol Mebus of Easton, Pennsylvania, bought their 100-year-old farmhouse they were surrounded by fields and woodlands, but soon afterward they were threatened by a housing development. Read how they solved their habitat problem.

on the back porch. A bird bath was filled daily. The stage was set.

Their efforts were rewarded: the wildlife responded. "In spite of the coming of the suburbs," Carol Mebus told us, "our backyard seems to be doing well. Deer appear in the middle of the afternoon to nibble on the grass growing on our upper three acres. Our list of birds has grown. Two skunks and two opossums make nightly forays to our back porch for table scraps. A local sparrow hawk tried to raid our oriole nest, but was driven off by the parents with the aid of a couple of grackles. Our feeders are emptied daily by the titmice, chickadees, house finches and cardinals. I can look out my kitchen window and see 'the family' of eleven young pheasants . . . usually in my zinnias. On the other side of the house a rabbit is munching on the shredded wheat biscuits I put out, and the 'sweet, sweet, sweet' of the song sparrow drifts through the window."

The Mebuses' interest in wildlife is contagious and eventually rubbed off on Mrs. Mebus's fifth-grade class at Paxinosa School. She enjoyed telling her students about her birds and the other wildlife they attracted to their yard. It is impossible to calculate what good things resulted from that learning experience.

"Perhaps that's what is wrong with a lot of people today," speculated Carol Mebus. "They are too far removed from nature. I have found that the natural world can be more calming than a tranquilizer and at the same time very invigorating. I have to live near nature; I could not be content to visit it for two weeks in the summer as so many people do," she concluded.

• *Tucson, Arizona:* When you live on the desert, as Vern Gwaltney does, the three basic needs of wildlife remain the same, but the emphasis shifts.

GWALTNEY YARD, TUCSON, ARIZONA

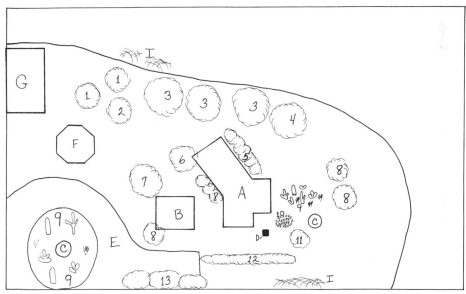

1. Palo verde	A. House
2. Pomegranate	B. Garage
3. Pecan	C. Water
4. Apricot	D. Feeder
5. Shrubs	E. Driveway
6. Orange	F. Guest house
7. Peach	G. Vegetable garden
8. Pyracantha	H. Natural desert
9. Cactus garden	vegetation
10. Strawberries	I. Brush pile
11. Acacia	
12. Oleanders	
13. Trees and shrubs	

Water is the key to success of this Tucson, Arizona, backyard habitat owned by Vern Gwaltney. By building two water holes fed by garden hoses, he attracted an amazing array of desert birdlife.

Mr. Gwaltney found out quickly that water was far more likely to bring wildlife to his yard than food or cover. His newly installed water holes with two dripping pipes met with immediate success. Within hours, Gwaltney was host to an array of desert wildlife ranging from gila monsters to owls, including three different species of hummingbirds and numerous other desert songbirds.

"The secret," says Gwaltney, "is the continuous availability of water, supplemented by feeders filled with a mixture of grain and bacon fat. Put all this in a setting of natural and planted desert cover and you have it."

• *Rhinelander, Wisconsin:* There are many reasons why people buy their houses, but a major consideration for Roy and Connie Hunter of Rhinelander, Wisconsin, was a wooded backyard along the Wisconsin River. It was a ready-made backyard wildlife habitat full of birds. Connie had become interested in feeding birds when they lived in a rented duplex only a quarter of a mile away from their new home. She knew the area was ideal for birds. The property they selected had everything required for a model bird sanctuary. There were mature birches, oaks, sugar maples and jack pines. Underneath there were many shrubs and vines including wild strawberries and black raspberries. The number of birds was impressive.

HUNTER YARD, RHINELANDER, WISCONSIN

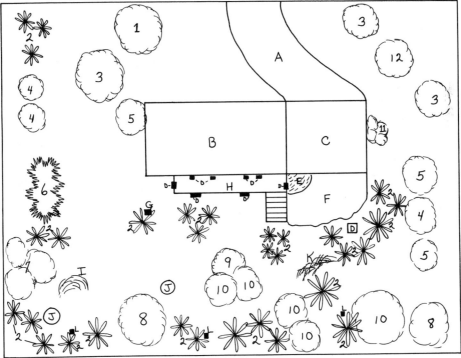

1. Mountain ash	A. Driveway
2. Jack pine	B. House
3. Crab apple	C. Garage
4. Red cherry	D. Seed feeder
5. Highbush cranberry	E. Waterfall
6. Cedars	F. Rock garden
7. Russian olive	G. Roosting box
8. Oak	H. Deck
9. Sugar maple	I. Compost pile
10. Birch	J. Bird bath
11. Clump oak	K. Brush pile
12. Rhododendron	L. Suet in tree

When Roy and Connie Hunter of Rhinelander, Wisconsin, selected a location for their new home, they also chose a ready-made birding habitat. Feeders on their upper deck are usually jammed with 200 or more birds every day.

Red-breasted nuthatches and chickadees are among the 15 species the Hunters feed in their backyard.

During the winter, when the Hunters have their upper deck lined with feeders, there are between 100 and 200 birds of some fifteen species on a typical day. Kit and I watched evening grosbeaks fight over the sunflower seeds in the Droll Yankee feeders, and blue jays—dozens of them—vie for space on the tray feeders. There were red-breasted and white-breasted nuthatches, hairy and downy woodpeckers, purple finches, chickadees and brown creepers.

Connie does something a little different with the chunks of suet she gets from her butcher. She puts them high in the crotch of a large tree, some distance away from the house. In another tree she hangs a large, suet-laden pine cone that she picked up in the Deep South.

In the summer Connie feeds orange marmalade to the orioles. During one three-week period, the orioles consumed fifteen pounds. She also supplies the orioles with string and yarn to help them with nest building.

Bird food gets expensive at the Hunter household, about $400 a year, she told us. But that includes the cost of Connie's special mixture of peanuts and peanut butter, Grape Nuts, rolled oats, wheat germ and bacon fat plus the wild bird seed mixture. The Hunters provide hundreds of pounds of sunflower seed most winters (sometimes fifty to sixty-five pounds a week when there are evening grosbeaks about).

Some of their unusual visitors include a bald eagle, a variety of ducks that waddle up from the river, screech owls and kingfishers. Strangely, they have no cardinals, sparrows or juncos.

To keep the birds from hitting windows across the back of their house, the Hunters have hung red ribbons from the top of the windows so that they float in the wind across the panes.

• *Des Plaines, Illinois:* We walked quietly along the woodland path. Pine needles were soft underfoot. Sunlight dappled the arching fronds of the ostrich fern. A wood thrush called and then darted through the undergrowth out of sight.

A north woods hike? No, just a stroll through another superb backyard wildlife habitat, this one at the home of Robert and Ellen Vanderpoel of Des Plaines, Illinois.

Twenty years ago, when the Vanderpoels moved into their sub-urban dwelling, the backyard was a giant weed patch without a single tree or bush to soften the harsh sunlight. But now, after thousands of hours of planning and planting and hard work, their

VANDERPOEL YARD, DES PLAINES, ILLINOIS

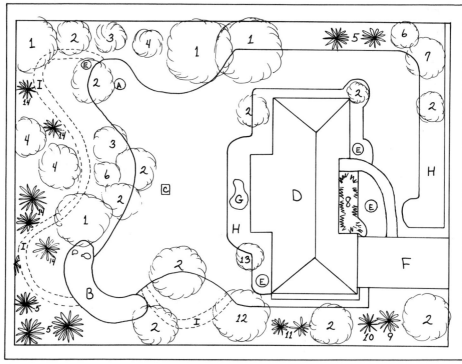

1. Pin oak	A. Bird bath
2. Crab apple	B. Fish pond
3. Red oak	C. Post feeder
4. Washington	D. House
hawthorn	E. Rock pool
5. White pine	F. Driveway
6. Shadblow	G. Rock garden
7. Maple	H. Pool
8. Yews	I. Path
9. Austrian pine	
10. Swiss stone pine	
11. Dwarf pine	
12. Mountain ash	
13. Flowering dogwood	
14. Spruce	

yard is a micro-woodland. Their three Norway spruce and four pin oaks tower 35 feet. Thick plantings of shrubs encircle the yard. An 18-foot-long fish pool planted with pond lilies provides a haven for sunfish and minnows . . . and a watering spot for birds.

The heart of the habitat is the "jungle," where a tangle of oak, spruce, crab apples, hawthorns and shrubs cover about one-fifth of the backyard area. A 70-foot-long path curves through the jungle, giving the feeling of being in a deep woods.

All of this natural habitat and food are supplemented in winter by one pole feeder and one Droll Yankee for cardinals, chickadees, purple finches, crossbills and evening grosbeaks. The Vanderpoels spread additional seed on the ground for mourning doves and juncos. The recent addition of a Niger seed feeder has drawn flocks of goldfinches, redpolls and pine siskins.

Bob told us, "May is the 'wild season,' the month when nature runs rampant. Our trees, a green haze in late April, are full of migrating warblers in May. Tiny flycatchers dart from exposed branches in hot pursuit of insects. Orioles and rose-breasted grosbeaks sing from the highest oaks."

This is not a north woods, just the superb backyard habitat of Robert and Ellen Vanderpoel in Des Plaines, Illinois. Twenty years ago, this was nothing more than a weed patch, but after thousands of hours of work, it has become a suburban micro-woodland.

Bob went on to tell us that the trickle of water at their pool is "maddeningly enticing" to many kinds of birds. In just twenty-five minutes last spring, he counted seven species of warblers at the pool.

By midsummer, the Vanderpoel yard is alive with families of robins, blue jays and mourning doves. "Last summer, the male cardinal stole the show," Bob told Kit. "While the female gallivanted about on her own, the male dutifully picked berries from our yews and crab apples, mashed the berries against our window sills and then fed them to its two waiting babies."

Bob Vanderpoel, news editor for the Chicago *Sun-Times*, has a philosophy about his backyard habitat: "There are a hundred ways a person can recharge his spiritual batteries and identify with nature. Our backyard sanctuary does the job for me."

• *Fairport, New York:* When the Charles Haines family moved into their new subdivision home in Fairport, New York, in 1971, there was nothing growing except a few mature trees at the back end of their ⅔-acre lot.

"This yard was virtually nude of any plant life or wildlife," Carolyn Haines told us on a bright day in October. "We missed seeing birds, so we decided to create a wildlife habitat here."

As we talked with Carolyn Haines, I glanced out her kitchen window. What a remarkable job Carolyn, Charles and their daughters, Marie and Karen, had done in just five and a half years!

1. Capitata yew	18. Sunburst locust	A. House
2. Japanese quince	19. Juniper	B. Patio
3. "Old-Fashion" crab	20. Viburnum	C. Feeder
4. Zuni crab	21. Arborvitae	D. Water
5. Rhododendron	22. Highbush cranberry	E. Vegetable garden
6. Euonymus	23. Forsythia	F. Rock pile
7. *Amalanchier canadensis*	24. Yew	G. Natural spring
8. Rose ramblers	25. Hopa crab apple	H. Creek
9. White oak	26. Redbud	I. Fence
10. Mountain ash	27. Fir	J. Compost pile
11. Russian mulberry	28. Weeping willow	
12. London plane tree	29. Wild apple	
13. Spruce	30. Cattails	
14. Strawberries	31. Native trees and shrubs	
15. Lilacs	32. Red raspberries	
16. Chinese maple	33. Autumn olive	
17. Potentilla	34. Native ferns	

HAINES YARD, FAIRPORT, NEW YORK

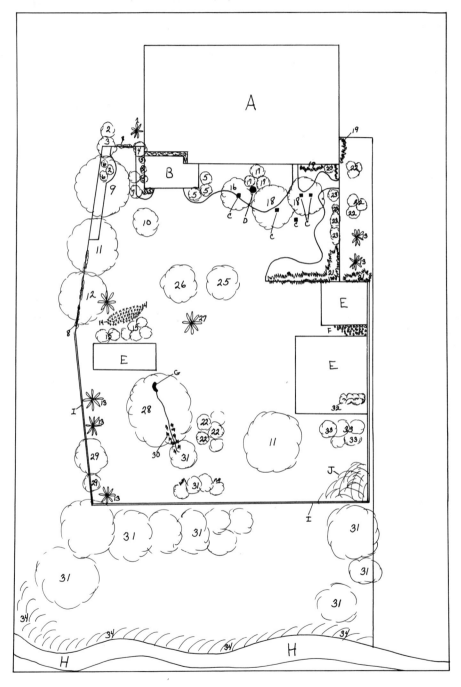

Carolyn Haines tells Kit about how they developed their Fairport, New York, backyard into a model wildlife area. Carolyn was so successful in her own yard that she now works for a local landscape firm designing other backyard habitats.

Surrounding their backyard patio was a garden planted in a multitude of annuals and perennials. There was rhododendron, arborvitae, viburnum, highbush cranberry, forsythia, euonymous, Japanese quince, daylilies, hostas and creeping myrtle. Mixed among the plant beds were several bird feeders and a bird bath, connected by a path of round wooden slabs.

Along the lot lines and on both sides of an attractive wooden fence were more small trees and shrubs: white spruce, Washington hawthorn, blue spruce, arborvitae and white oak. Several birdhouses were also there.

In the back half of their large yard were vegetable patches, rock piles, a compost pile, a garden shed and the girls' jungle gym. Near the back of the yard was a spring that seeped into the grass. Here the Haineses had created a miniature cattail marsh. At the back lot line, where the mature trees stand, the vegetation grows wild and a lovely little creek some three feet wide trickles across the property.

From no birds in 1971, the family bird list has grown to forty-one, including many breeding species. Some of the more unusual visitors include horned lark, mockingbird (rare that far north), and dickcissel. A red-tailed hawk that landed on the bird bath for a drink several years ago shocked all the songbirds . . . and Carolyn Haines, too.

There have been other kinds of successes. The Haines's yard has gained a local reputation, and each spring groups tour the yard to admire this total renovation of typical bare-tract subdivision land.

Carolyn's creativity in her own backyard led to designing backyard habitats in the yards of her friends and finally to a position as a horticulturalist with a local landscaping firm. She also spearheaded a move to have landscaping for wildlife included in a course offered at the Rochester Institute of Technology, where Charles was assistant provost.

We asked Carolyn how she decides what to plant and where to plant it.

"You must be aware of the land you are dealing with," she told us. "To attract wildlife, the trick is to make it look like it all grew there naturally."

• *The Dalles, Oregon:* Twenty-three years ago, when Dr. and Mrs. Robert Rice first saw their tract of land along Mill Creek, it was a truck farm where only a cock pheasant reigned supreme. Today it is a unique and well-vegetated wildlife woodland. The Rices built their home fifteen years ago between the road and the creek. It was designed for a maximum view of the creek and the woods that surrounded it. The Rices worked hard to cultivate the food and cover plants, like giant mullein, which the chickadees and downy woodpeckers enjoy. They transplanted wild currant and other shrubs from the woods and were given birches, staghorn sumac and Douglas firs to plant. They spent about $200 on trees and shrubs, and both the Rices and the birds have benefited greatly. "We always felt that our plantings were to be shared," Mrs. Rice told us. "We use some of the cherries, blackberries and elderberries, but the robins, black-headed grosbeaks and orioles probably eat more than we do," she added. The Rices enjoy the beauty of the wild roses, while

RICE YARD, THE DALLES, OREGON

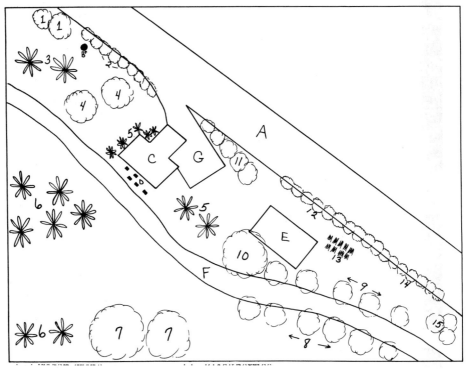

1. Oregon grape
2. Wild roses
3. Douglas fir
4. Gingko
5. Spruce
6. Ponderosa pine
7. Oak
8. Deciduous trees and thicket
9. Small creek trees and brush
10. Sycamore
11. Food-bearing shrubs
12. Blackberries
13. Cattails
14. Elderberries
15. Cherries

A. Unimproved street
B. Spring
C. House
D. Feeders
E. Vegetable garden
F. Creek
G. Driveway and parking area

the rufous-sided towhees find the rose hips to be tasty snacks each fall.

The bird feeders at the Rice home line the deck and hang from the trees above the creek. The birds that come to those feeders include such northwestern species as western tanagers, varied

When the Rices first saw their property on Mill Creek, The Dalles, Oregon, 20 years ago, it was a truck farm. Today it is a model wildlife area that is also home to many western species including black-headed grosbeaks, varied thrushes, western tanagers, violet-green swallows and Lewis's woodpeckers.

thrushes, black-headed grosbeaks, Bewick's wrens, violet-green swallows, Lewis's woodpeckers and California quail that eat under their Douglas fir trees. They also told us a dipper lives in the creek below the house.

"Sometimes we have to buy thirty to forty pounds of apples for the robins who get caught in a late snowstorm," Mrs. Rice told us.

One of the Rices' delights each summer is seeing the young downy woodpeckers at the suet and the young California quail scurrying through the ground cover with their parents.

The Rices have never put out birdhouses but have left many natural cavities for their birds to nest in. "Our project has been one of caring for and saving habitat rather than one of creating new habitat at great expense. Our reward is a peaceful oasis right in the middle of town with interesting wildlife right here at our back door," Mrs. Rice stated proudly.

• *Lake Wales, Florida:* Mountain Lake Sanctuary, the home of the Bok Singing Tower of Lake Wales, Florida, has a unique bird habitat. The so-called "Birdwatch" on the sanctuary grounds is not in a backyard, but it is built in such a way that it could be. For that reason we are including it in this section.

Kit and I visited the sanctuary in early January, when the numbers of wintering birds should have been at a peak. The Birdwatch is a small, lean-to–shaped building overlooking a lovely shallow pond, about one acre in size, surrounded by cattails, large cedar trees and one huge southern longleaf pine. Through a huge window we saw two wood duck boxes, one on a post in the water and one on the trunk of the pine. In the foreground were several stumps sticking out of the water and covered with songbird food. The water was so clear that we could see fish swimming in the shallows.

The numbers of birds attracted by this setup, however, were disappointing. Sanctuary Director Ken Morrison told us that there were fewer birds than usual but he could not explain why. We watched cardinals, blue jays, red-winged blackbirds and grackles feed at the stumps. We saw goldfinches and a Cooper's hawk flying over. A female towhee ate at the water's edge as did several gray squirrels and one raccoon. A pair of common gallinules swam in and out of the cattails.

The design and function of this setup is excellent. The pond was created by forming a large dish with a bulldozer, lining it with a

MOUNTAIN LAKE SANCTUARY BIRDWATCH, LAKE WALES, FLORIDA

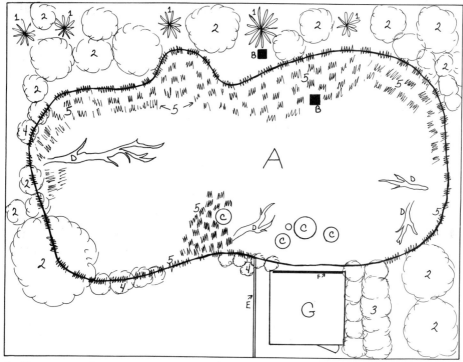

1. Various southern pines
2. Miscellaneous native deciduous trees
3. Dense hedge
4. Native shrubs
5. Cattails

A. Pond
B. Wood duck nesting box
C. Stump feeders in water
D. Dead tree
E. Fence
F. Viewing window
G. Birdwatch building

layer of clay and then a layer of macadam. Flooded and allowed to grow, the pond has a genuine wild look.

The viewing house is about 18 × 20 feet with a glass wall in front and a door in the back. It has a sand floor to minimize noises and a dark interior to conceal human movement. On the outside, thick vegetation grows away from both sides of the building to hide people as they enter and exit. Four rows of chairs inside permit twenty people to watch. It was an inviting setup, and it made Kit and me long for the day when we could duplicate it on our own property.

A man-made bird pond on the grounds of the Mountain Lake Sanctuary, Lake Wales, Florida, is one of the unique wildlife habitats in America. Seated in a viewing room called the Birdwatch, visitors are entertained by birds at the stump feeders, ducks in the cattails and other birds and mammals at the water's edge.

● *Thomasville, Georgia:* If there is such a thing as the "Best of the Best," the Number 1 Backyard Bird Window has to be at the home of Ed and Betty Komarek of Thomasville, Georgia.

When the Komareks bought "Birdsong Plantation" in 1939, it was in a sad state of disrepair, Betty told Kit and me. "From that day on," she said, "we redesigned Birdsong for the birds."

The Komareks have developed something far beyond a typical bird feeding station, or even a typical backyard wildlife habitat. They have designed a living picture, a pseudo-Japanese garden with

KOMAREK YARD, THOMASVILLE, GEORGIA

1. Pecan	12. Oregon grape	A. House
2. Yucca	13. Violets	B. Cypress stump feeder
3. Camellia	14. Cactus garden	C. Cypress knee feeder
4. Sabal or cabbage	15. Food-bearing shrub	D. Water
palm		E. Large rock
5. Aspidistra		F. Shallow pond
6. Crepe myrtle		G. Moss-covered boulder
7. Japanese plum		H. Moss-covered log
8. Carpinas		I. Rail fence
9. Ferns		J. Dust bath
10. Mulberry		K. Meadow
11. Flowering quince		

The world's best birding window has to be at the home of Betty and Ed Komarek of Thomasville, Georgia. The Komareks bought "Birdsong Plantation" 40 years ago and redesigned it into a bird watcher's paradise.

living, wild birds to provide the movement, all seen through a framing window.

"Come quietly," Betty whispered as we walked through the old farm kitchen to a middle room of the house. It was a bit of a shock to enter a darkened room and look through a glass wall onto a skillfully designed natural scene filled with pools, rocks, logs, shrubs, flowers, trees and birds, birds and more birds. Dozens of cardinals, blue jays, yellow-rumped (myrtle) and pine warblers, tufted titmice, Carolina wrens, goldfinches, chickadees and red-winged blackbirds filled the scene.

For years Betty has designed "wonder windows" for other backyard bird watchers in Georgia and Florida. The Mountain Lake Sanctuary "Birdwatch" at Lake Wales, Florida, is a product of her genius.

Betty Komarek designed this living picture, a pseudo-Japanese garden with wild birds to provide the movement in her yard. Kit and I spent several days photographing and enjoying the famous window.

"I do a landscape first, then I put in the feeders," Betty explained. "Birds give the scene movement," she told us. Her feeders are natural logs, stumps and a bamboo trough at the base of the window.

Kit and I spent several days sitting in Betty's darkened room, photographing and enjoying the activity on the other side of the glass. There was never a dull moment.

The scene had depth. Not only was the foreground well done with its lovely moss-covered rocks, cypress stumps and lush decorative shrubs, but the background was equally interesting. Through breaks in the plantings we could see a quarter of a mile in two directions over fields, rail fences, pecan groves and open woodlands.

"See that dead opossum way out there?" Betty asked. Sure enough, we could see a pile of light-colored fur lying about a thousand yards away in the pecan grove. "That's a roadkill Ed brought to me yesterday. The vultures will love it."

A short time later, both turkey and black vultures were circling

Dusting areas for birds are almost as popular as watering facilities. The dusting spot here is one of the many innovations in the Komarek habitat.

overhead and finally a young turkey vulture landed on the opossum. Her roadkills have also brought in foxes, a bobcat, crows and red-tailed hawks. Hawks, however, present some problems for the Komarek birds. Several times each day, when there are birds on every limb, rock and stump, panic suddenly strikes.

"Hawk!" Betty cried, as every songbird in sight disappeared. A female sharpshin landed and sat motionless on a limb for about ten minutes. During her visit, not another bird was seen.

It was nearly half an hour after the sharpy had gone that the first songbirds were back at the feeders. A little later, a male bobwhite quail scurried onto the scene followed by a covey of six others. Then a red-bellied woodpecker landed on the cypress stump, which contained nuggets of Betty's special bird dinner (cornmeal, peanut meal and suet). Brown thrashers, catbirds, mockingbirds and towhees all joined the crowd. Again the view through the window had at least fifty birds.

The noisiest of all the birds was the brown thrasher, who hammered at the food in the bamboo window tray. "Hear that pecking?" Betty shouted. "I've answered the front door more times than I care to admit because of that old boy," she laughed.

Over thirty-five years of living at Birdsong, Betty and Ed have had thousands of people visit their 15 × 18-foot viewing room. School classes, garden clubs, 4-H clubs, celebrities and many renowned ornithologists and bird photographers have paraded through the Komarek home. One woman was quoted as saying, "This visit has changed my life."

Indeed, the Komareks have undoubtedly changed many lives. It takes but a few moments at the window to demonstrate what can be done to bring the beauties of nature into people's lives.

AND THERE WERE OTHERS

• *Clio, Michigan:* When Marjorie McLaren built her home twenty-five years ago, she also established a wildlife habitat in her backyard. She has maintained and improved it during the years that followed. She provided mud, yarn and string as nesting material for robins and other species. The 20-foot span of her back lot remained unmowed and was allowed to grow wild. She built a recirculating waterfall, prodded neighbors into fixing up their yards for wildlife

An important feature of the backyard habitat of Marjorie McLaren of Clio, Michigan, is this recirculating water area. Located in the middle of a subdivision, the McLaren yard is home to dozens of birds as well as an occasional deer that also drinks from the pool.

and recently reported that there are more birds around than ever before, including some newcomers like flickers, mourning doves and rose-breasted grosbeaks.

• *Watertown, Wisconsin:* Jennine and Jacob Burbach reported seeing more and more songbirds with each new spring in their backyard wildlife habitat. They stopped cutting the undergrowth and have let their former flower garden grow wild. Though they live only 100 feet from a river, they felt that water was important enough to have a water area for birds installed closer to their house.

• *Hagerstown, Maryland:* The backyard habitat of retired science teacher and librarian Donald and Helen Haugh was so successful that they were asked to make personal appearances before service clubs and senior citizen groups to tell how they did it. They received letters of congratulations from the President of the United States, the Secretary of the Interior and the mayor of their city.

• *Auburn, Alabama:* When she was attending classes at Auburn University, Angeline Honnell enjoyed coming home for lunch to watch the birds from her enclosed patio. "It's like reviewing the troops," she told us. " 'How are you doing?' 'How much you have grown!' It just makes me feel good."

• *Pittsburgh, Pennsylvania:* When her husband died in 1973, Margaretha Roush's daughter and grandchildren helped complete a backyard wildlife habitat started by the Roushes. Even the neighbors pitched in to help build and maintain a model wildlife habitat that became a memorial to Mrs. Roush's husband.

• *Oak Grove, Louisiana:* It wasn't until Jim Lyons broke his ribs that he and his wife, Dorothy, discovered the joy of feeding birds in their backyard. After several years of improving the habitat on their property, the Lyonses had a great variety of birds, including a pair of screech owls. They maintained feeders on their window sill and around the yard. A newly built concrete bird pool attracted many more birds.

• *Sterling, Virginia:* The addition of food-producing shrubs and trees, dead pine trees, stumps and logs brought many new birds to the backyard habitat of the Carl Lewis family. The combination of new vegetation, a flowing creek 300 feet behind the property and a well-stocked feeding station made their project a huge success.

• *West Bend, Wisconsin:* Twenty years of loving care for a 20-acre tract near the center of West Bend has brought happiness and awards to Lawrence and Ann Maurin. They have identified 224 species living in their various habitats, including a 3-acre shallow lake bordered by cattails, wetland shrubs and open marsh. White cedar, Norway spruce, highbush cranberry and multiflora hedgerows are planted throughout the property. The local bird club recently identified 40 species of birds in one outing on the Maurin tract.

• *Myrtle Point, Oregon:* Another example of what can be done on a one-acre lot is the backyard of Ellen E. Endicott. She planted dozens of small trees, shrubs and a 45-yard hedge; installed a bird bath; built an 8 × 4-foot concrete pond, created brush piles, rock piles, and a wall of stone and brickwork. The birds also enjoyed the dusting areas she established. Not only is her yard frequented by all the common songbirds of that area, but she also sees deer, quail, skunks and rabbits. Last summer she used 10 pounds of sugar to feed the hummingbirds sugar water.

• *El Paso, Texas:* Just ten minutes' walk from downtown El Paso is a little oasis of tropical plants, natural habitat, food and water for birds. It is at the home of Mrs. G. L. Wratten, one of the first certi-

Just a 10-minute walk from downtown El Paso, Texas, is this tropical oasis in the backyard of Mrs. G. L. Wratten. It may be the only refuge for birds in all of the business district of that large city.

fied backyards in the National Wildlife Federation's Backyard Wildlife Habitat Program. By planting trees, shrubs and cacti, and by taking tropical indoor plants outdoors in the summer, Mrs. Wratten created an ideal birding area in her 60 × 120-foot yard. "We are about the only place in the downtown area of El Paso for birds and small animals to find refuge," she told us. Her yard is enhanced by a concrete kidney-shaped pool, 2 × 6 × 1 feet, which is kept full by a dripping hose. Bird baths, brush piles, rock piles and stone walls complete the Wratten habitat, which lists roadrunners, Gamble's quail, rock wrens and nighthawks among its frequent visitors.

Given the right kind of natural habitat, birds like barn swallows, robins and phoebes will use the protected areas of buildings for their nesting locations.

BUILD YOUR OWN

Now that you have read how others have built successful backyard bird habitats, why not try it yourself? It is not hard to do and the rewards are many.

For those readers who have already established a habitat, perhaps this chapter has given you new ideas for improving your yard and your enjoyment of birds.

3
How to Build a Feeding Station

THE WINTER night was ending as I peered through the large window to our patio. The outside thermometer read eight degrees below zero. A light wind made little whirlpools in the snow, and in the first dim light a flock of juncos and tree sparrows was eating the seed I had put out the previous night. As the gray Wisconsin dawn progressed, a chickadee darted down from the linden tree, landed on the homemade salad-bowl feeder, selected a sunflower seed and returned to its perch. I watched the chickadee place the seed between its feet and hammer the edge with its sharp black beak. I counted fifteen taps before the shell split. The tiny bird scooped out the meat, dropped the husks and flew back to the feeder for more.

Even in the dead of winter in Wisconsin, many birds remain active and undaunted by the cold. But unless they have the luxury of a feeding station, they must forage over large areas to survive. Some do not survive. If, however, their basic needs are satisfied in one place, such as at a feeding station, they will congregate there in above-average numbers. That is surely true in our backyard, where we provide the three essential ingredients, supplemented by a year-round feeding station. On a good day in winter, we have recorded as many as twenty different species and more than one hundred individual birds. Often, as many as fifty birds visit the feeders at one time, including brown creepers, tree, white-crowned, white-throated and fox sparrows, crossbills, purple finches, goldfinches,

The salad bowl feeder containing sunflower seeds is a favorite of the chickadees. The tiny birds usually take one seed at a time to a nearby tree and then hammer the shell until it breaks and releases the meat.

redpolls, cardinals, chickadees, juncos, mourning doves, blue jays and six species of woodpeckers.

As I watched the chickadee eat that sunflower seed, it occurred to me that each species of seed eater has its own way of opening and eating sunflower seeds. The neighborhood bully, the blue jay, came in next and swallowed a dozen or more unshelled sunflower seeds before leaving. I suspected that it coughed them up later for cracking and eating.

Next, a nuthatch took a sunflower seed, flew to the linden tree and wedged it into the bark of the trunk. With the seed tightly locked, as in a vice, the nuthatch then struck the shell with its long bill until the treasure inside was his.

Another regular visitor, a female cardinal, arrived next. As usual, she preceded the male, reminding me of the does and fawns that pass my deer stand ahead of the more cautious buck. As soon as the female cardinal began to feed, the male joined her.

The cardinals attacked sunflower seeds in a totally different way. Standing in one place at the feeders, "Big Red" and his "Lady with the Lipstick" rotated the seeds around in their heavy nutcracker-

The male cardinal often arrives at my feeding station only after the female has preceded him, indicating that the coast is clear. Cardinals crack sunflower seeds with their heavy nutcracker-like bills.

like bills until they were just right for the squeeze that crushed the shells and released the goodies.

I watched the goldfinches, siskins and redpolls do their thing on the sunflower seeds in still another way, which was to "mouth" the seed until it broke.

The sunflower seed scenario was just one of many points of interest I saw that frigid morning from the warm side of the glass. By the time the winter sun was fully up, the whole patio was alive with birds.

Because we watch some of the same birds feed day after day, we have become attached to certain individuals. When we first spotted

Squirrels and blue jays are usually the tough guys at the feeding station, but the pine siskins can be just as feisty. Though they usually descend upon feeding stations in small flocks, they dislike sharing food, even with other siskins . . .

a one-legged junco, we thought it was just warming the other leg in its belly feathers. But that wasn't the case. "Long John Silver" seemed just as healthy as the others, but he had to do his hopping on one leg instead of two. He was there with the others as my morning with the birds continued.

Squirrels and blue jays are the usual tough guys of the feeding station gang, but on this particular morning, the feisty pine siskins were causing the biggest ruckus. Those gutsy little birds were intimidating any bird feeding within pecking distance regardless of size. In a typical exchange, the siskin spread its brown mottled wings, crouched in a threatening pose and wheezed at its adversary.

. . . these tiny northern invaders can be very aggressive, even toward each other.

This aggressive behavior would become more pronounced as spring approached. One of my neighbors had seen a siskin peck a goldfinch on the head and pull some of its feathers out.

It was in the middle of one such siskin scrap that Kit announced breakfast was ready. We eat most of our meals at the windows so that we can continue to watch all the happenings.

It should be obvious to the reader by now that our feeding station is center stage at our home, from the moment we awaken until dark—and sometimes into the night. I'm sure some people consider us a little strange because we are so involved in watching the birds in our backyard, but I feel our preoccupation has become more and more accepted as people all over America discover the fun and happiness they can have with the birds every day.

An elderly neighbor of ours lost her husband last year and became so depressed that she found herself with nothing to do and nothing to live for. Almost out of desperation, I took a bird feeder to her, placed it outside her kitchen window, filled it with wild bird seed mixture and suggested that she keep her eye on it.

Within a month, that woman had a whole new interest in life. She began calling me several times a week with the latest news about her feeding station, which soon expanded to five feeders. One day I thought she was having a heart attack as she told me that five redpolls were eating her sunflower seeds at that moment, and I should come over immediately to see them.

Another neighbor, a middle-aged man who has been divorced for many years, had been curious about our feeding station and decided to set one up in his own yard. The first year or so he maintained several seed feeders on a picnic table in his lower yard, some distance from the house. When he complained to me one day about not seeing much activity at his feeders, I suggested that he move the whole operation closer to his house, near his office window. "There is no use in having a feeding station if you can't see what is happening," I told him. Dutifully, he moved his feeders to his office window, where there were more trees and shrubs to provide cover. He set up a beef suet feeder, a Niger seed cylinder and two sunflower seed containers. What a difference! The next thing I heard was his complaint that he couldn't get his work done because there was always so much happening outside his window.

One of the most unusual feeding stations I know of was maintained for years by a couple on Captiva Island, Florida. Every day at noon, the lady of the house put out table scraps for her wildlife friends, who just happened to be several dozen black and turkey vultures that gathered in the trees of her backyard every morning awaiting their handout. Skeptical visitors were quickly told that scavenger birds can be just as fascinating to watch as songbirds.

It is not an exaggeration to say that people's lives have been totally changed by their fascination for the birds they have attracted. A growing army of backyard bird watchers is turning to this kind of family recreation as a wholesome and rewarding kind of human experience. The Amherst researchers mentioned in chapter 2 also found that back in 1972, twenty percent of the U.S. households purchased an average of sixty pounds of bird seed per year. Some of the breakdowns by city for that year appear in the accompanying table.

City	Percentage of households that fed birds	Pounds of seed purchased per household
Boston	23.8	69.6
Cleveland	24.7	57.6
Milwaukee	19.4	64.5
New York	15.1	49.2
St. Louis	19.8	64.5

HOW TO SET UP A FEEDING STATION

It's easy to set up a feeding station. All you need is a little food and a feeder or two. But knowing what kind of food to put out, where to put it and how to make it easy for the birds to find can be the difference between a successful feeding station and one that is only occasionally visited.

Take another look at your backyard, or whatever place you think is best for setting up your feeding station. We have found that there are at least four feeding niches to be filled at any feeding station: Ground level, table-top, hanging and tree trunk.

• *Ground level:* Ground-eating species such as sparrows, juncos, mourning doves, quail, pheasants and towhees don't really care where you put the food. They would just as soon eat it off the ground. However, to keep the feeding area tidy and the seed from blowing around, we use a split fireplace log, flat side up. If the flat

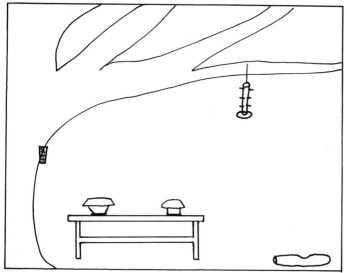

There are four major feeding niches at every feeding station: (1) ground level; (2) table-top height, which includes low post feeders; (3) hanging and high post feeders; and finally, (4) tree-trunk zones. Backyard bird watchers who fill all four niches should attract the greatest variety of birds to their feeders.

Ground feeders will be just as happy to have their food thrown right on the ground, but split logs, trays and other ground-level receptacles will help keep the feeding area tidy and protected from the wind.

side has a little cup or groove in it, all the better for holding the food. We place our logs along the outside edge of the patio near a little shrub or spruce tree to provide cover. During heavy snow-storms, when the ground feeders are buried, it is often best to throw the seed right on the snow where the birds can find it quickly. Snow cover will not be a problem if you place the feeders where they will have overhead protection. Our second-story balcony provides an overhang that shields the food from most snowstorms.

• *Table-top level:* A picnic table, bench or windowsill, which gets the food off the ground a few feet, will attract cardinals, chickadees, titmice, wrens, blue jays, blackbirds, grosbeaks and many others. By using a tray or wicker basket on the table, you keep the seed from blowing away. Wicker is good because it allows water to drain. If you use a tray or bowl, be sure that it has holes in the bottom to allow drainage so that the food will not be soaked. Seed containers

Table-top feeding birds like this yellow-rumped (myrtle) warbler seem to feel comfortable eating on top of a stump, picnic table or a low post feeder. Yellowrumps are particularly fond of fruit.

Post feeders also attract yellowrumps, particularly if you give them bird cakes. Hyde's Jr. Bird Feeder is a good all-around feeder for a variety of birds.

mounted on low posts at table height should attract those same species that feed a few feet off the ground. Post feeders come in many models from any of dozens of bird feeder manufacturers. We have several staggered around the perimeter of our patio, and we vary the height of the posts to add more variety to our offerings.

• *Hanging feeders:* As with post feeders, there are dozens of models available at lawn and garden centers, supermarkets and department stores everywhere. The Droll Yankee Company of Foster, Rhode Island; Welles Bishop Company of Meriden, Connecticut; Heath Manufacturing Company of Coopersville, Michigan; and Hyde's, Inc., of Waltham, Massachusetts, are among the leading companies that manufacture the best hanging and post feeders.

Hanging feeders like this Droll Yankee are particularly well suited for gold-finches, other finches, chickadees, grosbeaks, nuthatches and cardinals, which feel comfortable on feeders that swing with the wind. Not all species, including some of the undesirables, like these kinds of feeders.

The hanging feeder is the most popular with people, though not necessarily the most popular with birds. Most hanging seed feeders blow in the wind and are generally unsteady. Because of this they attract only those species that can hold on while eating—chickadees, titmice, nuthatches and the finches. The most effective of all hanging feeders are the Niger seed cylinders and stockings, which we will explore later in this chapter. It is best to suspend them from tree limbs because the tree provides the cover and security birds need.

To photograph various kinds of hanging feeders, we had a lightweight chain stretched from our balcony to the linden tree and back to the balcony. Large links allow us to snap on as many hanging feeders as we want without having them bunch up against each other in a strong wind. Some feeders were hung on the chain among the tree branches, while others were placed in the open. We have had as many as nineteen feeders up at one time!

● *Tree trunk sites:* Aimed primarily at the woodpeckers, the tree trunk feeders usually contain suet, bird cakes or peanut butter and are nailed against the trunk of a tree at eye level or a little higher. Woodpeckers cling to the tree bark while feeding. Brown creepers, chickadees, titmice, jays and even crows will visit the tree trunk

Beef suet at tree-trunk level is the preferred food and location for woodpeckers. My "suet tree" attracts four species of woodpeckers regularly and two others on occasion.

Commercially made feeders are for sale in most lawn and garden centers, hardware stores and discount houses. Most are the hanging types, but there are also post, table-top and tree-trunk models. They cost from $5 to $30.

feeders. Any kind of mesh bag, even an old onion bag that is tied shut, can be used. Wire mesh works well and keeps raccoons from stealing the suet.

My practice of attracting birds to the four niches or feeding levels has its exceptions. Some species, such as chickadees, will feed at all four, but generally each species has its preferred level. If the station provides a choice of all four feeding levels, a greater variety and a greater number of each species should be attracted. Try it.

HOMEMADE FEEDERS ARE FUN AND COST NOTHING

It isn't necessary to buy expensive feeders to have a successful feeding station. Birds really don't care if you spend $30 for a redwood barn feeder or if you scrounge something from the attic or the woods. The attractiveness of a bird feeder satisfies people more than birds.

• *Seed feeders:* Because we prefer natural-looking feeders, we find that something from the woods is always attractive and costs noth-

Backyard bird watchers don't have to spend money for feeders. This split log is one of the most popular on my patio. Its natural look enhances the appearance of the feeding station, as well as this photograph of a female purple finch.

A unique idea in homemade feeders is this one made of two auto hubcaps joined by a metal dowel. Read the end of this chapter for information about the safe use of metal feeders.

Homemade Niger seed feeders like this one can be made out of a plastic mailing tube, a coffee can lid and wooden dowels. Tiny holes, pierced in the mailing tube, allow enough room for the goldfinches to extract the seed.

ing but a little effort. We have discussed the split log, but another possibility is a whole log or a stump with a depression or cavity in it. Laid on its side or anchored straight up, it will hold seed nicely. We have found that birds seem to feel more at home when sitting and eating on natural feeders. These feeders from the woods can be placed on picnic tables or benches or even hung from a tree for the table-top species. Seed feeders can also be made from wicker baskets, beer trays, wooden boxes and cinder blocks stacked with openings on the side for ground or table-top use. Hanging feeders can be made from two wooden salad bowls with a dowel between them or two hubcaps with a metal dowel between them, plastic and paper milk cartons, and coconut shells. A friend of ours who works for an art studio in Sheboygan, Wisconsin, designed a homemade variation of the Niger seed or sunflower seed cylinder from a clear plastic mailing tube. Corn cobs impaled on a nail or an old-fashioned corn dryer also make attractive feeders.

• *Suet feeders:* Birders devise all kinds of homemade feeders to hold

The best suet feeder is made of a lobsterman's bait bag. A white-breasted nuthatch in my yard was a frequent visitor.

Clothes hangers bent to the right shape and joined by wire make an interesting hanging suet feeder for downy woodpeckers and others.

Hardware cloth shaped around a coffee can lid and fitted with a wooden perch makes another good feeder for suet-eating birds like this downy woodpecker.

suet. By bending coat hangers into a pear-shaped holder, wired together, a large suet feeder can be made. Another simple design calls for hardware cloth to be curved to the shape of a two-pound coffee can, using a plastic coffee can lid as the bottom. A wooden perch is wired through the hardware cloth at the base. For the "natural" look, cut little logs about two or three inches in diameter and about a foot long. Drill one-inch holes halfway through the logs and stuff suet or bird cake into the holes. Hang the new feeder in a tree. Still another idea is to set a dead tree into concrete and drill holes in it for suet. This works even better as a summer feeder because the lack of foliage on the dead tree allows better observation of the feeding birds. Our southern friends use cypress trees and cypress knees for this purpose. They are very attractive to both bird and human eyes. A pine cone, particularly the large kind that grows in

In the South, cypress knees are adapted as feeders when holes are drilled in the sides for suet or bird cake. This feeder was photographed in the Komarek habitat in Thomasville, Georgia.

Still another natural suet feeder is a sawed-off tree limb or stick with 1-inch holes drilled in the sides. Either pure suet or bird cake can be forced into the holes for birds that enjoy the tree-trunk-level feeders.

Large pine cones from southern and western pine species dipped in melted bird cake make attractive feeders for downy woodpeckers.

the Deep South and in the West, makes an interesting feeder for suet-eating birds. Merely dip the cone into hot rendered suet or bird cake mixture, then chill it to harden. The pine cone feeder hanging from a nearby limb is very pretty.

WILD BIRD SEED MIXTURE

The most popular and one of the least expensive wild bird foods is the "wild bird seed mixture," a combination of eight to ten differ-

Most wild bird seed mixtures contain 8–10 different kinds of seed, but research shows that most birds eat only 4 of the varieties and the remaining seed is wasted.

A plastic milk bottle can be made into a handy scoop for bird seed.

ent varieties of seeds usually including cracked corn, sunflower seed, red millet, white millet, milo, oat groats, wheat and one or two other seeds. The additional seeds often depend on the location of the mill and the kind of seed available in that area. Wild bird seed mixtures in the South will have more southern grains, such as rice, compared to the northern mills, which are more likely to use buckwheat and other northern varieties. These mixtures are packaged in five- and ten-pound bags and are sold in most grocery stores under different labels. They usually are available in fifty-pound bags from feed mills, lawn and garden centers and some hardware stores. I have found that by purchasing the wild bird seed mixtures in fifty-pound bags I save money, as the per-pound price is considerably lower.

During an interview with the owner of a Milwaukee milling company that mixes and bags its own wild bird seed, I asked why they had selected the particular eight varieties of seed used for their mixture: cracked corn, sunflower seed, red and white millet, milo, oat groats, wheat and buckwheat. His answer was not very satisfactory. He said that he had been in the poultry feed business all his life and he knew that size and attractiveness had been the determining factors with poultry. He concluded that all birds were the same, and he had selected these eight varieties based on those criteria.

I pressed him further by asking if he had ever done any experimenting with the mixture. He said no, but agreed to allow me to conduct an experiment and offered to provide bags of unmixed seed.

Slinger, Wisconsin, Seed Survey

Jessie Rapp, a friend of ours in the local Audubon Society, volunteered to conduct the first tests at her home in Slinger, Wisconsin, to determine which birds like what seeds. We also wanted to find out if all eight kinds were being eaten. By building a buffet tray 18 feet long with separate, lift-out baskets for each of the eight varieties, Jessie was able to monitor the kinds and amounts of seeds her birds ate from the trays over a two-week period in mid-April. She found that cracked corn, sunflower seeds, and red and white millet were the preferred fare. Her birds, which included cardinals, chickadees, goldfinches, white-breasted nuthatches, blue jays, juncos, red-winged blackbirds, purple finches, song sparrows, flickers, white-crowned sparrows, vesper sparrows, cowbirds, red-bellied woodpeckers and an oriole, did not touch the buckwheat nor the milo, and only juncos, red-winged blackbirds and one oriole ate wheat. Surprisingly, the first bird to visit the trays, a chickadee, sampled all eight kinds before settling on cracked corn as its first choice.

Rubicon, Wisconsin, Seed Survey

We ran the same test nearly a year later with another Audubon friend, Nancy Andrich of Rubicon, Wisconsin. This time, it was colder and there was snow on the ground. Nancy monitored the birds and what they ate over a two-week period in January and again during two weeks in late March and early April. She found that the four most popular seeds in the wild bird seed mixture were sunflower seeds (a resounding first place), followed by white millet, red millet and cracked corn. There was some interest in milo, but little or no interest in buckwheat, oat groats or wheat. Twice as much sunflower seed was eaten as the next most popular seed. Nancy's

Screech Owl

Goldfinches

Purple Finch

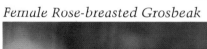

Female Rose-breasted Grosbeak

Bluebird

Tufted Titmouse

American Robin

House Wren

Evening Grosbeak

Cardinal

Meadowlark

Gray Catbird

Red-shouldered Hawk

Northern Oriole

Red-headed Woodpecker

Yellow-rumped Warbler

Jessie Rapp of Slinger, Wisconsin, fills bird seed study trays to determine which seeds are eaten by what species of bird.

To keep the seeds from getting soggy, each experimental seed survey tray had a window screen bottom for drainage. Wheat was one of the least desired seeds in the mixture tested.

A second bird seed survey was conducted for this book by Nancy Andrich of Rubicon, Wisconsin. Though the two studies led to the same conclusions, the Andrich survey showed that twice as much sunflower seed was eaten as any other, but that more species of birds ate cracked corn.

reports show that the following species ate sunflower: goldfinches, purple finches, chickadees, redpolls, blue jays, nuthatches, tree sparrows, juncos, house sparrows and grackles. The two millets were eaten by tree sparrows, juncos, house sparrows and, in the spring, song sparrows and cowbirds. Cracked corn was enjoyed by all the birds, including mourning doves. Though more sunflower seeds were consumed, more species ate cracked corn.

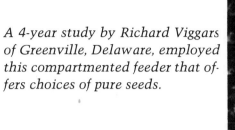

A 4-year study by Richard Viggars of Greenville, Delaware, employed this compartmented feeder that offers choices of pure seeds.

Greenville, Delaware (Viggars), Seed Survey

An in-depth four-year seed survey was conducted by Richard M. Viggars of the Pennyfeather Corporation in Greenville, Delaware. Using the sixteen different kinds of seed most often fed to birds (including those in the wild bird seed mixtures), Viggars studied what seeds were eaten most often and the species that ate them. He designed a compartmented feeder for the tests, placing pure, unmixed seeds of each variety in separate compartments. His studies with seven commercial mixtures showed that they were composed of from forty-two to seventy-six percent of seeds that birds would not take, and a number of seeds birds favor were not present. The feeder as well as more information about the survey are for sale through the Pennyfeather Corporation, Box 3861, Greenville, Delaware 19807.

CONCLUSIONS OF THE VIGGARS SURVEY:

1. The wheat used in commercial mixtures was a complete waste, as none was accepted in the four years.
2. Milo was almost as useless, with only 3 lbs. in every 1,000 lbs. of total seeds being eaten.
3. Red millet was little better, with only 13 lbs. in 1,000 lbs. taken.

4. Sunflower (domestic black stripe) and white millet were better suited to birds' tastes, though gray-striped sunflower is preferred over black-striped, with less waste. More recent tests on several kinds of sunflower make it clear that old or carry-over seed that had dried out was usually ignored if fresh seeds were available.

5. Peanut hearts are an excellent cool and cold weather food when offered unmixed. They will attract several species of insect and berry eaters, including catbirds and mockingbirds.

6. Crushed hulled oats are a good songbird food, but only when mixed with peanut hearts.

7. Yellow corn (fine cracked) proved to be a highly acceptable, low-cost feed, but not in hot weather.

8. Canary seed (Moroccan and Argentine) was very acceptable, and along with the Niger thistle and dwarf or yellow millet attracted several species of the finch family.

9. Hulled whole oats (oat groats) were disappointing, with only 9 lbs. per 1,000 lbs. accepted.

10. Broken white rice, sterilized hemp and buckwheat were used in the tests, but were not accepted by the birds.

11. White or proso millet was a good general food for a wide range of birds at any time of the year, but there were times when they turned to pearl millet and/or small golden millet for a change. Of the small millets, foxtail was the least accepted.

Based on this survey and on his many years as a professional backyard bird watcher, Richard Viggars compiled the following list of species and their food preferences in the Middle Atlantic states:

Blue jay	Sunflower seed, peanut hearts, bacon dripping cups, cracked corn
Cardinal	Sunflower seed, cracked corn, millet
Crossbill	Sunflower seed
Black-capped and Carolina chickadee	Sunflower seed, suet, bacon dripping cups, peanut hearts, canary seed
Mourning dove	Corn, millet, hulled sunflower seed, Niger
Common flicker	Suet, peanut hearts
American goldfinch, house finch, purple finch, pine siskin	Niger seed, sunflower seed, peanut hearts
Evening and rose-breasted grosbeak	Sunflower seed, peanut hearts, cracked corn
Ruby-throated hummingbird	1 part sugar to 4 parts water mixture with Protein Nectar
Red-breasted and white-breasted nuthatch	Bacon dripping cups, sunflower seed, suet, peanut hearts
Northern (Baltimore) oriole	1 part sugar to 4 parts water, orange halves
Common redpoll	Millet, corn, canary seed

Field, house, song, white-crowned and white-throated sparrow	Millet, cracked corn, sunflower kernels, canary seed
Tufted titmouse	Sunflower seed, suet, bacon dripping cups, peanut hearts, canary seed
Rufous-sided towhee	Millet, cracked corn, peanut hearts, sunflower kernels, canary seed
Downy, hairy and red-bellied woodpecker	Sunflower seed, suet, bacon dripping cups, peanut hearts
Carolina wren	Bacon dripping cups, peanut hearts, golden millet, dried fruit

I believe these tests send a loud and clear message. If you have certain favorite species that you want to attract to your feeders, these surveys show the way. Selective feeding will also help you to discourage the undesirable birds.

SUNFLOWER FOR THE PRETTY BIRDS

It is obvious that sunflower seeds are the best all-around food for attracting the greatest number of desirable birds. It is a preferred fare among cardinals, blue jays, chickadees, the finches, the grosbeaks, titmice, the nuthatches and crossbills. Of the many kinds of sunflower seeds, gray-striped is most readily eaten by birds, though

Sunflower seeds are eaten with gusto at most feeding stations. Northern invaders such as evening grosbeaks, redpolls, pine siskins, pine grosbeaks as well as purple finches (shown) will consume large quantities of sunflower if the backyard bird watcher offers it.

Sunflower seeds in bubble feeders or the similar satellite feeders are eaten primarily by the agile species like the goldfinch (shown) as well as other finches and chickadees. House sparrows and starlings are more adapted to well-anchored post or ground feeders.

all are popular. Sunflower seeds are sold in grocery stores in five- and ten-pound bags, but the fifty-pound bags from feed mills and lawn and garden centers bring down the average cost per pound considerably.

NIGER, THE NEWEST AND MOST SELECTIVE SEEDS

The most selective, most exciting and newest bird seed to come along in my lifetime is Niger, often erroneously called thistle, seed. This tiny black import from India and Africa has been a canary food for years, but only in the last half decade has it been bagged for wild birds. It is dynamite for finches!

Dwight M. Brown of the George W. Hill Company, Florence, Kentucky, reports that "our purchases and sales of Niger seed over the last five years have been phenomenal. They have increased perhaps as much as tenfold." Until 1974, Reinders Brothers of Elm Grove,

Wisconsin, didn't handle Niger seed. Now they sell ten to twelve tons a year.

Until you have tried Niger (or thistle seed) you cannot imagine how popular it can be among finches. We heard about it from friends who gave us a Niger seed sock feeder and a supply of seed. It took a week or so before our goldfinches found it and tried it, but once they became hooked, they were with us every day, all day, throughout the entire year, even during the breeding season. Purple finches, pine siskins and redpolls are also big Niger seed eaters; it seems that none of them can ever get enough.

Hyde's, Inc., of Waltham, Massachusetts, makes some of the best, least expensive Niger seed feeders. One is the Distlefink, a plastic cylinder with six tiny holes above six perches. Their best is the Seed Silo because it distributes equal amounts of Niger to three compartments. We normally have two or three Hyde Niger seed feeders in use throughout the winter, which gives us a maximum capacity of eighteen birds eating at the same time. They are always jammed with goldfinches, redpolls and siskins. Every perch is filled, and other birds flutter in midair trying to get on. I counted forty gold-

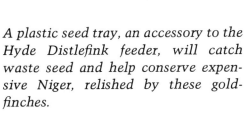

A plastic seed tray, an accessory to the Hyde Distlefink feeder, will catch waste seed and help conserve expensive Niger, relished by these goldfinches.

Goldfinch males become bright yellow again as spring passes into full bloom. Backyard bird watchers can look for other, more subtle changes in the birds at their feeders.

A close-up of the Seed Silo shows two redpolls eyeing the sky and the ground for danger.

finches at or near the feeders one day, and seventy redpolls on another day.

The success of Niger seed as a bird food is absolutely amazing, and we recommend that every backyard bird watcher try it. It is more expensive than sunflower, but each seed is so tiny that a pound goes much farther. Purchase it in large quantities to save on the per-pound rate.

Recently, Niger has been harder to buy and has tripled in cost due to embargos by the countries that grow it. For these reasons, some birders are diluting the pure Niger with flax, canary seed and rape. Nevertheless, birds tested with diluted mixtures preferred pure Niger seed. Dick Viggars of Pennyfeather Corporation in Greenville, Delaware, found that a 50-50 mixture of black Niger and wild canary worked well. He also says that hulled sunflower seed or sunflower chips are an acceptable substitute for Niger, though they cannot be fed in Niger seed feeders.

FINCH MIX DOESN'T BEAT PURE NIGER

Because of the enormous increases in the cost of pure Niger seed, feed companies have been bagging what they call "finch mix,"

Because of the exorbitantly high cost of Niger seed, seed companies are now packaging a mixture they call "finch mix" consisting of eight kinds of tiny seeds including some Niger but costing only half the price of the pure "black gold." Finches will eat it but much prefer the pure Niger.

which includes thistle, or Niger. It also includes other tiny seeds such as canary seed, German millet, black lettuce, dwarf essex rape, flax and hemp. It sells for half the price of pure Niger. We tried it and found that the finches will eat it *if* pure Niger is not available. But given a choice, there is no doubt about what they love—they'll take the black gold every time.

SUET FOR INSECT EATERS

Another very popular bird food is beef suet, the dry, white, hard beef fat available at most butcher counters (usually free to good customers). Suet, containing protein and fats, supplies birds with quick energy. It is best placed in a mesh bag, which can be either an old onion bag or a commercially made suet bag. One of the best makeshift suet bags, however, is the nylon mesh bag that lobster fishermen use as a bait bag in their traps. There are also a great many metal or wire mesh suet holders available at stores that sell bird seed feeders.

The suet bag should be hung against the trunk of a large tree so that woodpeckers can eat while holding onto the bark of the tree. Some backyard bird watchers like to hang an additional bag in mid-air from a branch or the eaves of their house for chickadees.

Beef suet, available from meat counters (free to good customers), is an important feeding station food. It is the preferred fare of the wood-peckers but is also eaten by most other species. Suet is just as popular during the summer months as in winter.

In Rhinelander, Wisconsin, the Hunters put their suet high in a tree crotch for birds such as these blue jays.

Suet is the favorite food of the woodpecker clan. We have six species of woodpeckers eating on our suet tree almost daily: hairy, downy, red-headed, flicker, yellow-bellied sapsucker and red-bellied woodpeckers. Apparently suet is a good substitute for the insects woodpeckers find in nature. We have noticed that a great many of the seed-eating birds will also eat suet occasionally, particularly during cold weather. Chickadees, nuthatches, titmice, blue jays, starlings and even cardinals will surprise us with their occasional visits to the suet feeders.

We have discovered that the suet feeder we maintain the year around is the most consistent attraction in our station. Suet usually lasts several weeks, it is easy to replenish and it is attractive to woodpeckers and other species, winter and summer.

OFFER A SMORGASBORD

We like to experiment with different kinds of food.
• *Fruit cup:* Kit keeps our grapefruit rinds and fills them with small chunks of citrus, apple, berries and sometimes banana. Placed out where it can be seen, but close enough to cover to allow birds a

Fruit cups made of grapefruit rinds and filled with a mixture of fresh fruits and berries are worth trying on migrating warblers, thrushes, wrens, tanagers and grosbeaks as they pass through your area.

feeling of safety, the fruit cup is relished by orioles, thrushes, catbirds, thrashers, tanagers, a number of warblers and wrens. Some people use dates, figs, prunes and raisins in their fruit cups and find them readily accepted.

• *Other seeds and nuts:* Just about any kind of nuts or nutmeats—almonds, black walnuts, English walnuts, hickory nuts, pecans—are devoured by certain species of birds. Peanut hearts, whole peanuts and peanut butter are also very popular, as are the seeds of melons and pumpkins. Popcorn, scratch feed, whole corn and cornmeal are very good, but will also attract the less desirable species. Safflower seed is said to be the ideal cardinal food, but our cardinals have never agreed with that.

Different foods for different birds. Here my son Peter smashes Georgia pecans to feed to Wisconsin birds in late winter.

● *Some oddball foods:* Just for the fun of it, try some of these on your birds: cheese, bakery products like doughnuts and cakes and cookies, dry cereal, coconut, cornbread, cracker crumbs, dog biscuits and dry dog food, cooked eggs, cooked oatmeal, ears of frozen sweet corn and watermelon pulp.

● *Grit:* Most birds need a certain amount of grit in their diet for grinding food and for its mineral value. Put fine gravel, egg shells, fireplace ashes, sand or ground seashells in a bowl or box near the food. Pet stores and feed mills sell poultry or canary grit, which is fine for wild birds.

● *Salt:* It seems that all animals are attracted to salt, and it just might be popular at your feeding station. A coarse salt is best.

RECIPES FOR HOMEMADE BIRD CAKES

There is a great deal of interest among backyard bird watchers in concocting their own special bird cakes using combinations of ren-

There are hundreds of recipes for bird cakes, but most contain rendered suet, peanut butter and cornmeal. Allowed to harden in cupcake papers or a muffin tin, they are easy to handle for feeding to the birds.

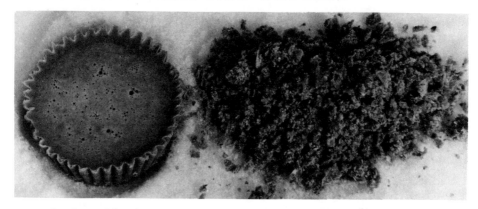

Some backyard bird watchers set out unbroken bird cakes; others crumble the cakes, or force them into holes in trees or stumps. Still others hang them in mesh bags.

dered suet, bacon grease, peanut butter, cornmeal and bird seed in a mixture that hardens and can be forced into cavities, placed in feeders or merely crumbled and set out. Kit has tried many of the recipes and has settled on the following all-around bird cake mixture for general use:

One part peanut butter   Six parts cornmeal
One part melted beef suet

Spoon into paper-lined muffin tins and cool. When hardened, cakes may be removed from the tins and stored frozen until needed.

There are many others you might like to try. Donna Suther of Britton, South Dakota 57430, has assembled many of these interesting recipes into a fascinating little booklet she titled "Feed Your Feathered Friends." The following are just a few of the recipes in her booklet:

CUPCAKES

1 lb. suet in small pieces   1 c. yellow cornmeal
1 c. chunk-style peanut butter   1 c. mixed wild bird seed
1 c. rolled oats   1 c. sunflower seed

Melt suet over low flame until fried out. Stir other ingredients into fat until blended. Pour into paper cupcake cups placed in muffin pans. Chill until hardened; remove paper and put in your wire suet basket.

MAGIC MEATBALLS

2 c. bread crumbs
½ lb. ground suet
3 chopped apples (seeds and all)
½ c. flour
1 c. sugar

¼ c. cornmeal
1 handful nutmeats
2 handfuls raisins
1 8-oz. jar peanut butter
1 c. wild bird seed

Mix these ingredients together; add enough melted bacon drippings to hold everything together. Shape into balls, or press into pine cones and hang from the branches of a tree. Can be frozen for future feedings.

Mrs. Belle Shaw, Idaho
Mrs. J. T. Rickets, Idaho
Mrs. Kenneth W. Stadler, Idaho

MILK CARTON FEEDER

Render ½ lb. beef suet per feeder in double boiler. Stir often. Cool after removing membrane. Add 2 or 3 T. sand and crushed eggshells. Before it thickens, add old toast, broken into small pieces. Then add seeds—saffron, sunflower, cracked corn, millet and milo. Pour mixture into milk carton feeders to a depth of 2 in. or more. Put a flat stone in feeder, then finish filling with mixture. Cool and cut out holes for feeding on two sides before hanging out for birds.

COCONUT SHELL FEEDER FILLER

3 scooped-out coconut shells
3 c. suet or other hard fat,
    ground
1 c. yellow cornmeal
1 c. raisins, currants or
    cranberries

1 c. coarse brown sugar
1 c. flour, white or brown
1 c. bird seed or nuts or dry
    cereal
1 c. chunky peanut butter
Water (not too much)

Combine ingredients. Add enough water to make the consistency of porridge. Cook over hot water until blended and smooth. Fill coconut shells or other containers ¾ full. Chill. Hang on branch near window. Woodpeckers, nuthatches and chickadees love it.

Mrs. Mildred Pettit
Brookton, Maine

OAT CAKE DELIGHT

½ c. ground wheat or Roman meal
½ c. rolled oats
1 egg

2 T. New Orleans molasses
½ c. whole milk
1 T. cooking oil

Blend all together and beat well. Pour mixture into an oiled pie pan and bake at 350° until a golden brown. Raisins may be added, if wished. Crumble well when placed on feeder.

Mrs. Irma S. McElroy
Milton-Freewater, Oregon

ORANGE FEEDER FOR ORIOLES

A special feeder that holds two halves of an orange or grapefruit has proved a success in attracting not only orioles, but catbirds, robins and others.

PINE CONE FEEDER

Combine rendered suet, bacon fat, peanut butter, cornmeal and wild bird seed. Pour the mixture over large pine cones, filling in all the crevices. Hang cones on branches. Mixture can be poured in small pans and other ingredients added, such as nutmeats, raisins, chopped apples, cracked corn, bits of meat, cereal.

Mrs. Harold G. Phillips
Kingston, Pennsylvania

RAISIN CAKE FOR THE BIRDS

1 c. cornmeal
1 c. uncooked oatmeal
1 c. flour
1 c. wheat germ

1 c. raisins
½ c. fat (unsalted)
1 c. skim milk (dry milk okay)
½ tsp. baking soda (if you wish)

A few bread crumbs may be added, but are not necessary.

Mix all ingredients to form a thick batter. Add raisins dredged with flour. Grease the pan well and flour lightly. Bake at 350° for about an hour. Cool and break up into good-sized pieces. Place chunks in mesh bags and hang in shrubs.

Mrs. J. E. Thome
Auburn, California

The birds' shishkabob consists of suet, peanuts, orange halves, doughnuts and apples. Hung from a branch of a tree near the feeding station, this concoction can be very interesting to some birds.

SHISHKABOB

String pieces of bread, doughnuts, cornbread, meat scraps, biscuits, apples, oranges, raisins or any type of dried fruit on 3- or 4-foot lengths of twine. Drape over tree branches.

Mr. and Mrs. Earl Atkinson
Salt Lake City, Utah

Nearly all the birds that frequent your feeding station will enjoy these recipes. There is something for each of them . . . the seed eaters, the insect eaters and even those that turn up their bills at conventional bird foods. Try some of them and see if they aren't a hit in your backyard.

THE PASSING SPRING PARADE

Spring is a fascinating time at the feeding station because it signals the changing behavior of many birds. Sparrows and juncos become restless and temperamental. The male cardinal will begin to pass sunflower seeds to his lady. All the male birds tune up their songs and the male goldfinches change from drab olive to bright yellow, appearing a bit blotched in the process. It is during this same period that the female cowbirds arrive with their entourage of courting males.

Early spring is also the time for another invasion of redpolls, purple finches, siskins, evening grosbeaks and other migrants from the South. Though they are just passing through, big seed eaters like these make great inroads into the sunflower seeds because natural food is in shortest supply. One bird watcher reported that he had to stop feeding evening grosbeaks by mid-April because they also ate the buds of his apple trees.

One day in April, a friend told us about seeing eight unfamiliar brown-striped birds in his pear tree eating the small blossoms. Only after the males appeared did he realize that his pear tree was hosting eight pairs of rose-breasted grosbeaks. He put out sunflower seeds and the birds found them. The grosbeaks stayed around his home for over a month before continuing their journey north.

It is also in early April that the regular winter residents begin to disappear. The juncos, however, stay until May, the last to leave in the spring and first to return in the fall.

THE SUMMER FEEDING STATION

Obviously, the birds need more help finding food in winter than they do in summer, but that doesn't preclude having a summer feeding station. In fact, the summer feeding station presents experiences that winter-only feeders miss.

We take down most of the feeders in late April or early May. We leave the suet feeder on the tree trunk, one or two sunflower seed feeders and one Niger seed cylinder. That combination of feeders, the recirculating pond and lots of natural cover makes our patio an interesting and busy place for us to watch birds while we eat our meals, entertain guests, read or take wildlife photographs.

Because the goldfinches are late nesters, they maintain a heavy schedule at the Niger seed feeder right through the spring and well into the summer. Even when they are nesting and defending territories, the patio seems to be a common ground for at least three or four pairs. They do seem to be more aggressive during the warmer

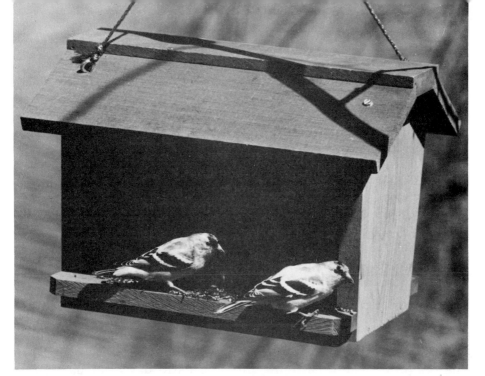

Through spring and into summer, goldfinches continue to feed on Niger and sunflower. The feeding station seems to be a common ground, even for competing males like these two.

Red-headed woodpeckers are usually seen at suet feeders, but this rare photograph of a redhead on a seed feeder shows that they are curious creatures.

months than at other times of the year, but they also manage to share the Niger seed.

The suet feeder is an interesting spot to watch in summer. Woodpeckers never seem to get enough suet, and even during the periods when they are feeding young, they are in and out of the feeder dozens of times a day. When the youngsters have fledged, they, too, visit the suet with their parents. It was interesting one summer morning to watch downy woodpecker adults show their young how to eat suet. The whole family of seven flew to the tree trunk next to the feeder. First the adults went to the suet and ate. Then one took a piece of suet to a youngster who was watching intently. They fed one or two of the closest progeny and then went back to the suet and ate more themselves. Eventually, the youngsters caught on and soon they, too, were eating at the feeder.

The same behavior was observed with the chickadee family. Last summer, the adults and what seemed to be an amazing number of youngsters all came barreling into the patio day after day. Some flew to the sunflower seeds, but most went to the suet. There were chickadees "dee-dee-dee-deeing" all over the place . . . and we loved it. We have enjoyed families of hairy woodpeckers and white-breasted nuthatches at the suet feeder as well.

Action at the summer feeding station is most rewarding as parent birds bring in their youngsters for the first time. Families of chickadees, nuthatches, downy and hairy woodpeckers are among those seen at this suet tree.

Incidentally, some people are afraid to put out suet during warm weather. They say it melts or rots. This has not been our experience. It works just as well in summer as it does in winter.

It seems to us that our birds are somewhat tamer in the summer. That may be because we are out with them during warm months and they get used to seeing humans close by. The downies are particularly tame, and it is not unusual for them to provide entertainment when we have dinner guests. We can stand within a few feet of the suet and watch them feed. Their little talkative noises, uttered while gorging themselves, add another dimension that we miss in winter when windows and doors are closed.

So, we recommend that you carry on a limited feeding program during the summer and reap some of the real joys of having birds in your backyard.

SUGAR WATER FOR HUMMERS

Hummingbirds are "suckers" for trumpet vines and impatiens blossoms, but a sure-fire way to attract them, particularly in the West, is with a sugar water feeder.

Summer feeding stations in the West and Southwest feature sugar water for hummingbirds. This black-chinned hummingbird was photographed at Mile Hi Ranch in Ramsey Canyon, Arizona, the Hummingbird Capital of the world.

In the East we have only the ruby-throated hummingbird, which is not as receptive to the sugar water as western species, but it will drink it. In the West, however, where there are as many as twelve species of hummingbirds to attract, sugar water is very popular. Our trips to Estes Park, Colorado, are highlighted by the sights of broadtailed hummingbirds flocking to sugar water feeders. The YMCA of the Rockies at Estes Park is one of the best places in Colorado to see broadtails at sugar water feeders.

The hummingbird capital of the United States, however, is Mile Hi Ranch, a facility of The Nature Conservancy in Ramsey Canyon near Sierra Vista, Arizona. The dozens of sugar water feeders hanging outside guest cabins at Mile Hi have flocks of hummingbirds of at least six species on any given day. Altogether, twelve species have been recorded there. The management fills the feeders every few hours and the birds consume an average of two gallons a day!

If you have ever seen a hummingbird in your backyard, we suggest that you try hanging a sugar water feeder near the flower beds.

Summertime is sugar water time at feeding stations, particularly in the West. A mixture of 1 part sugar to 3 or 4 parts water is guzzled by as many as 12 different kinds of hummingbirds at Mile Hi Ranch.

The feeders are available from lawn and garden centers everywhere. Homemade feeders need be no more than a glass jar tilted at a 45-degree angle, hung in a tree or from a post, and filled with sugar water. You may be surprised at the other species of birds that drink sugar water. Orioles, grosbeaks, warblers and tanagers are fond of the sweet liquid.

The mixture that we use is 1 part sugar to 3 or 4 parts water. We also like to add red food coloring (the safe kind), though it is not necessary. It is believed that the red color helps attract the birds' attention, though I can't prove it.

I have heard that sugar water is not good for the hummingbird's liver and that honey is better. However, all authorities I have talked to about this say that sugar water, mixed as directed, will not harm the birds, and that honey is more questionable. In any event, if you can get hummingbirds to come to your backyard for sugar water, you will have something very special.

DECORATE A BIRD CHRISTMAS TREE

Every December we decorate two Christmas trees, one for us indoors and one for the birds at the edge of the patio. The outside

The tradition of decorating the birds' Christmas tree dates back to the 16th century in northern Europe. Many backyard bird watchers enjoy hanging bird food on trees to feed those living feathered ornaments of red, blue and gold.

tree is a Norway spruce with edible decorations hung on it as a holiday treat for the birds. This is a custom dating back to the sixteenth century in northern Europe, where people honored the birds and beasts of the Nativity. Our ornaments consist of stale bread, peanuts, suet, popcorn, marshmallows, doughnuts, chunks of fruit and cranberries. Some of these goodies are hung on the boughs and some are strung together with a large needle and heavy thread and draped like a garland. The decorated strings give the tree a more festive look and they help keep the food from falling. We dip small pine cones in Kit's favorite bird cake recipe and hang them on the tree as well.

The birds' Christmas tree need not be an evergreen. It can be any kind of tree that is close enough for good observation and strong enough to hold the food.

What a great feeling we get when the birds' Christmas tree is laden with snow, goodies and brightly colored birds, which are the best decorations of all!

BIRD FEEDING—FACT AND FICTION

I have been writing about feeding birds for many years, and each time I do an article for a major magazine I get letters from readers criticizing me for not warning against the use of metal feeders on which birds can freeze their feet and eyeballs. Another point on which they take me to task is not warning about feeding birds peanut butter, which my readers believe will get stuck in their throats, causing death. Finally, they want me to tell everyone that once you start a feeding station in winter, you can't go away and leave the birds to starve.

Following a recent article I did for *National Wildlife,* I again received many letters about these same so-called problems. To try to quell these myths, I wrote to the Cornell Laboratory of Ornithology and asked for someone to respond to these people in a follow-up article in *National Wildlife.* Here is what Assistant Director Sam Weeks wrote:

> Over the years I have heard many "rules" of bird feeding—often things you must never do. Some of these are rather silly and were easily dismissed until, more and more, they were picked up and reproduced in a growing number of books on the subject. Now even more people are quoting these dictates.

After years of being criticized for showing photographs of birds at metal feeders, I asked the Cornell Laboratory of Ornithology to dispel the idea that birds' eyes and feet stick to metal in cold weather. The response is at the end of this chapter.

Perhaps it is time to do away with some of the myths associated with the practice of feeding birds.

First, one should realize that a well-operated feeding station may be the last stopping place for birds that are diseased or injured. Your food sanctuary may add another day or two to the life of such a bird. Thus, when you find a dead bird at or near your feeder, don't assume that it was somehow your fault. Many people think that the seed is contaminated, for instance, and want it analyzed immediately.

Freak accidents sometimes occur at feeders, perhaps partly due to the fact that a sick bird may spend more time there. Since a few birds have been seen with their feet frozen to a metal object, we are told never to use a feeder with metal on it. People who have felt the catch of cold metal freezing to their moist hands are quick to pick this up. But birds' feet are normally dry; and it is only in very rare situations, usually combining peculiar weather and a sick bird, that such freezing takes place. Indeed, under such conditions I have found a bird frozen to a *wooden* perch.

An incident which received much mileage was that of an unfortunate bird, again probably not in the best of health, whose moist eye membrane happened to make contact with, and freeze to, some metal. Birds, however, do not normally allow their eyes to touch foreign objects any more than we do. These really rare incidents have been reported over and over until they sound as common as the common cold. A well-designed bird feeder kept fairly clean and free from moldy seeds, with or without metal, has a much better safety record than most devices used by mankind.

The cause of death of small songbirds has sometimes been attributed to peanut butter, the birds presumably choking to death. It is more likely, however, that the bird's last meal was peanut butter, which was found in its mouth when the stricken bird was examined. Of the thousands of birds to which I have fed, and have seen feeding on, peanut butter, none have shown any signs of distress other than wiping their bills.

Some people attempt to put seeds into suet cakes. Birds feeding on suet need protein in addition to the fat. It is best to add high protein materials, such as canned dog food, dehydrated eggs, or peanut butter, to suet cakes rather than adding seeds.

Finally, it is often said, "Once you start feeding you must not stop until winter is over." And one sometimes hears its corollary, "Since I am unable to feed regularly this winter, I'm not going to start." Continuous and regular feeding certainly facilitates winter foraging for the birds and gives one a larger and more satisfying avian clientele, but they are equipped to make it without you. Most birds living in northern winters have evolved ways to exploit everchanging food resources. There is no single, localized, natural source which is guaranteed to last them all winter and they search out, often in flocks, new sources. As a matter of fact, a reserve does not have to run out for them to look elsewhere; birds will practically abandon a feeder when a period of unusually mild winter weather makes wild foods temporarily available again.

If you plan to be away from home and cannot find anyone to keep your feeder well stocked, then ease off on the quantities you feed before you leave. Barring a coincidental heavy snowstorm and cold weather, birds will find other food sources and will locate your full feeders again when you return.

WORTH IT ALL

As I have been writing this chapter, I have been constantly in the company of some seventy redpolls, only a few feet away, on the other side of the glass. Even when I wasn't watching them, I could hear their little chatter as they vied for positions on the Niger seed feeders. Some might wonder if these noisy little creatures were a distraction to me as I tried to concentrate on my work. No. As a matter of fact, they were a source of contentment.

Some of the photographs that illustrate this chapter were also made during this period as I was writing the text. I had my camera set up on a tripod for weeks in March and April, and each time the light was right and the birds were abundant, I'd take time away from the desk work to shoot a few more photographs.

Though backyard bird watching is a profession with us as well as a hobby, our experiences, even during the writing of this chapter, should be encouraging to those who are considering a feeding station of their own. It is an enormously satisfying endeavor. We certainly encourage you to try it.

4

A Birdhouse Can Be a Home

As a boy growing up in the household of a wildlife motion picture producer, I made frequent trips to my grandfather's farm in Butler County, Pennsylvania, some thirty minutes from home. We went to the farm often to photograph many kinds of wildlife that thrived there. Most vivid in my memory are the bluebirds that nested in birdhouses my dad had built and erected on fence posts dotting the 137-acre tract. I remember how he spent days in blinds recording on film the life history of those beautiful creatures.

During the ensuing years, I often wondered how the bluebirds at the farm were faring. National concern for the survival of that species led me to believe they probably had gone the way of so many of their kind.

Last summer, when Kit and I were in western Pennsylvania photographing tree swallows and wrens (which also nest in birdhouses), the bluebirds of the farm came to mind. We needed to photograph bluebirds, but no one in Pittsburgh, where we were working, could find one for us. Then it occurred to me that there might possibly be some bluebirds still nesting at the farm. It was only two hours away, and the drive was worth the gamble.

It had been twenty-five years since I had visited the old farm and as we topped the hill that overlooked it, my heart leaped. There it was, just the way I recalled.

Knocking on the door, I was delighted to find that the present

About two dozen species of eastern birds and a similar number in the West will nest in man-made birdhouses. The trick is to place the right kind of house in the right location for the species you want to nest in your backyard.

owner was the same man to whom my grandfather had sold the property many years ago. He remembered me and I him.

"Do you still have bluebirds?" I queried.

"Yep, there's a few still around," he answered. He went on to tell us that a young researcher had replaced our old bluebird houses some years back with new ones, but that even the new houses were now in bad shape.

Kit and I were eager to check the birdhouses, and our farmer

My childhood memories of the bluebirds nesting at my grandfather's farm paved the way for a second generation of Harrisons to photograph those lovely creatures at the same location 25 years later.

Many families of bluebirds have come and gone at "the Farm," but their progeny survives there today, thanks to the birdhouses.

friend offered to drive us around his property in a pick-up truck. We found about eight houses, three of which had active nests, but only one had baby bluebirds inside. We also found a fence post with a natural cavity nest filled with bluebirds. What a great feeling to find that the bluebirds were still there! They were probably the progeny of the same birds I had known as a boy. Perhaps their very survival had depended upon the houses we had left there, plus the new ones erected later. The only house with youngsters in it was a surprisingly new one, and just as my father had done twenty-five years earlier, we photographed the parents bringing in food.

Houses for bluebirds are important to the survival of the species. Bluebirds' natural nesting sites, tree cavities, are scarce. There used to be many in old orchards, but with the advent of steel fence posts and modern farming and forestry practices, hollow trees are at a premium. The house sparrow and starling usually win any battle for the occupancy of the few natural cavities and nesting boxes available to bluebirds. The use of DDT and other chlorinated hydrocarbons after World War II and severe winter weather have also had a profound effect on this insect-eating creature, adding up to a precarious situation for the species. Attention to the need for more bluebird houses and restrictions on the use of chemical pesticides should help the bluebird, but the situation is still in doubt.

In some areas of the East, "Bluebird Trails" were established where bird groups built and erected houses along hundreds of miles of back roads. Though bluebirds are not common inhabitants of the typical backyard, yours might be one of the lucky ones if you live in a rural or semirural area.

The dimensions of the bluebird house, size of the hole and where the box is placed are important, and you should refer to the chart on pages 166–67 before building a house for any species. Bluebirds are but one of about two dozen species of eastern birds that use nesting houses, or boxes (see chart for list). A similar number are also found in the West. Many of these species can be attracted to urban or suburban backyards, if the right kind of nesting boxes are provided. So, the use of birdhouses in the overall backyard habitat is important and can contribute significantly to the enjoyment of birds in your backyard.

To give you an idea of the demand for birdhouses, we built a wood duck house and erected it 30 feet high in a linden tree on our terrace.

Bluebird house dimensions are very specific. This cedar log house, sold commercially in stores, was well suited for this family of bluebirds nesting in western Pennsylvania.

Living on a small lake and having seen wood ducks searching for a nesting site in that tree, we felt reasonably confident that we would have wood ducks in our box the first year. We were wrong. The wood ducks never looked at it. But starlings and house sparrows did. It was a frustrating spring, watching the starlings and house sparrows fighting over our beautiful wood duck house, which was ten times too large for either species.

The demand for bird housing can be quite high. This wood duck house
was occupied by a pair of screech owls, several gray squirrels and a family
of wood ducks all in one 6-month period between October and April.

When fall came, we decided to leave the big box in the tree figuring that gray squirrels would use it. They did, but not on a regular basis. On the evening of October 26, just as it was getting dark, we noticed a head in the entrance of the wood duck house. With binoculars, we discovered to our great joy that it was a screech owl—the gray phase. It was there every morning and evening for several days. On the third day, we were surprised again to see another screech owl in the entrance—this one a red phase. Did we have a pair and would they nest in the box?

Not really. We saw the screech owls in the entrance only a few more times during the winter. But imagine our surprise when, on the morning of April 19, we saw a female wood duck sitting in the entrance hole. After a few minutes, she flew out of the box and into the marsh. The following day we watched her do the same thing. In fact, she repeated that routine four days in a row. It was not until the following week that we saw both wood ducks flying to the nesting box. The female disappeared into the house while the male circled out over the lake and then disappeared into the marsh. On Memorial Day Sunday, thirty-nine days after first seeing the hen, we watched sixteen ducklings pour out of the nesting box, drop 30 feet to the ground and disappear as they followed her to the safety of the marsh.

DIFFERENT HOUSES FOR DIFFERENT BIRDS

The most important thing to keep in mind when selecting a bird box for your yard is that each species has its own special requirements. The shape of the box, the diameter of the entrance hole and the location of the birdhouse will determine the kind of birds that will reside in it. For example, wrens, the most common backyard resident, prefer a small house with a one-inch entrance hole, hung in a tree and surrounded by cover, while a bluebird requires a larger hole and must have its house in the open.

The problem of having the undesirable species like house sparrows and starlings take up residence in your flicker box or martin house is ever-present. Use the specific requirements shown in the chart on pages 166–67 to help keep out the undesirable species. Perches on the fronts of the houses are unnecessary for most species, and eliminating them will help to further discourage house sparrows, who prefer the perch.

COMMERCIAL BIRDHOUSES

The same lawn and garden centers, hardware stores and house-wares departments that sell bird feeders sell birdhouses and shelters. They are made by the same reputable manufacturers and most are attractive and sturdy. A great many of the commercially made birdhouses, however, are designed only for wrens, bluebirds and chickadees, though a few manufacturers still build larger boxes for flickers, wood ducks and purple martins. Some manufacturers also make robin shelters. The smaller houses cost less than $10; the larger ones cost up to $30 and some, such as martin houses, well over $100.

Before buying a commercial birdhouse, decide first what species

Commercially made houses cost from $5 to over $100 each. But they cost little or nothing when made in the family workshop. Check the dimensions on the chart and try building some next winter.

HOW TO PUT THE RIGHT HOUSE FOR THE RIGHT BIRD IN THE RIGHT PLACE

Each bird species that will use man-made birdhouses occupies a particular ecological niche. This preference for a nesting site must be considered when building and placing birdhouses to attract specific species.

Likelihood code:
1. *Easiest birds to attract*
2. *Suburbs*
3. *Rural or estate*
4. *Special habitat*

The best colors for birdhouses are earth tones—in light shades that will keep the birdhouse from getting too hot inside: gray, flat green, light brown, tan.

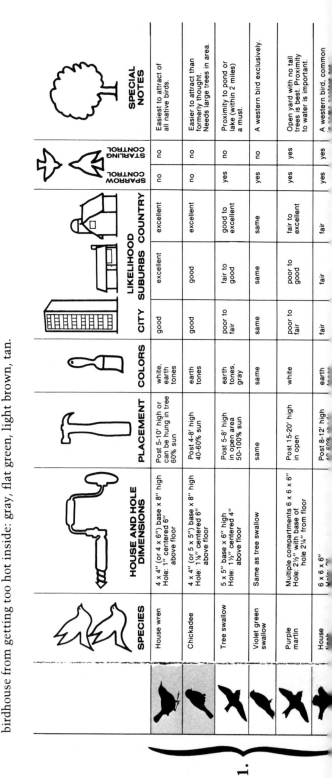

SPECIES	HOUSE AND HOLE DIMENSIONS	PLACEMENT	COLORS	LIKELIHOOD CITY	SUBURBS	COUNTRY	SPARROW CONTROL	STARLING CONTROL	SPECIAL NOTES
House wren	4 x 4'' (or 4 x 6'') base x 8'' high Hole: 1'' centered 6'' above floor	Post 5-10' high or can be hung in tree 60% sun	white, earth tones	good	excellent	excellent	no	no	Easiest to attract of all native birds.
Chickadee	4 x 4'' (or 5 x 5'') base x 8'' high Hole: 1⅛'' centered 6'' above floor	Post 4-8' high 40-60% sun	earth tones	good	good	excellent	no	no	Easier to attract than formerly thought. Needs large trees in area.
Tree swallow	5 x 5' base x 6'' high Hole: 1½'' centered 4'' above floor	Post 5-8' high in open area 50-100% sun	earth tones, gray	poor to fair	fair to good	good to excellent	yes	no	Proximity to pond or lake (within 2 miles) a must.
Violet green swallow	Same as tree swallow	same	same	same	same	same	yes	no	A western bird exclusively.
Purple martin	Multiple compartments 6 x 6 x 6'' Hole: 2½'' with base of hole 2¼'' from floor	Post 15-20' high in open	white	poor to fair	poor to good	fair to excellent	yes	yes	Open yard with no tall trees is best. Proximity to water is important.
House finch	6 x 6 x 6'' Hole: 2''	Post 8-12' high 40-60% sun	earth tones	fair	fair	fair	yes	yes	A western bird, common in …

1.

Species	Box dimensions	Placement	Color						Comments
Bluebird	5 x 5" base x 8" high Hole: 1½" centered 6" above floor	Post 3-5' high in the open, sunny	earth tones	poor	fair	excellent	yes	no	Likes open areas, especially facing a field.
Bewick's wren	4 x 4" base x 8" high Hole: 1¼"	Post 6-10' high 50% sun	earth tones	fair	good	excellent	yes	no	Likes thickets, hedges.
Tufted titmouse	4 x 4" base x 8" high Hole: 1¼"	Post 4-10' high sun or shade	earth tones	fair	fair to good	excellent	yes	no	Prefers to be near or in wooded areas.
Flicker	7 x 7" base x 18" high Hole: 2½" centered 14" above floor	Post 8-20' high	earth tones	fair	good	good	yes	yes	Needs 4" sawdust for nesting.
Carolina wren	4 x 4" base x 8" high Hole: 1½"	Post 6-10' high sun or shade	earth tones	poor	fair	good	yes	no	Prefers proximity to thick underbrush.
Nuthatch	4 x 4" base x 10" high Hole: 1¼" centered 7½" above floor	Post 12-25' high on tree limb	like a natural cavity	poor	poor	fair	yes	no	Should be covered with bark.
Downy woodpecker	Same as nuthatch Hole: 1¼"	same	same	poor	poor	poor	yes	no	Prefers own excavations. Needs sawdust for nesting material.
Hairy woodpecker	6 x 6" base x 15" high Hole: 1½"	Same as nuthatch	same	poor	poor	poor	yes	no	Same as nuthatch.
Crested flycatcher	6 x 6" base x 15" high Hole: 2" centered 6-8" from floor	8-20' high on post or tree limb shade preferred	simulate woodpecker cavity	poor	poor	fair	yes	yes	Needs secluded, private spot. Should be covered with bark.
Red-headed woodpecker	Same as crested flycatcher	same	same	poor	poor	fair	yes	yes	Needs sawdust for nesting material.
Wood duck	10 x 10" base x 24" high. Hole: should be an ellipse 4" wide x 3" high centered 20" above floor; this excludes most raccoons	On post 2-5' over water or on tree 12-40' high. Hole should face water	earth tones	poor	poor	good	no	yes	Shavings or sawdust 3-4" needed for nesting. If wetlands or lake within ¼ mile, wood duck will explore most nearby habitat.
Sparrow hawk	Same as wood duck	same	same	poor	poor	fair	no	yes	Open approach needed; box should be on edge of woodlot or in isolated tree.
Screech owl	Same as wood duck	same	same	poor	poor	fair	no	yes	Prefers open woods or edge of woodlots.
Saw-whet owl	Same as flicker	same	same	poor	poor	fair	no	yes	
Robin / Barn swallow / Phoebe	6 x 6" base x 8" high Roof required for rain protection	On side of building or on arbor	earth tones, wood	fair / poor / poor	fair / fair / fair	fair / excellent / fair	no	no	Use is irregular. Prefers open country. Likes water best.

2. 3. 4.

Nesting Platforms:

you want to attract to your yard, then check the chart on pages 166–167 for the dimensions. Armed with this information, you can make your purchases intelligently.

HOMEMADE BIRDHOUSES

One of the best winter indoor activities for families is the building of birdhouses. About the time you are ordering seeds for the family garden, you'll also want to consider the needs of the birds in your yard for the upcoming nesting season.

Birdhouse building can also be a scout project, a nature center effort or a school shop project. As you build the houses, again, keep in mind the dimensions and colors recommended in the chart on pages 166–67. Additional plans for birdhouses are usually available from your state conservation department or county agent.

We sometimes purchase our birdhouses and feeders from the local Easter Seal Homecraft Store. They will build the houses to our specifications, the cost is minimal and, by having them do it, we are helping their cause, too.

I erected this house with great hope that some flickers would move in. However, one pair of starlings after another fought over the box until one finally raised a family in it.

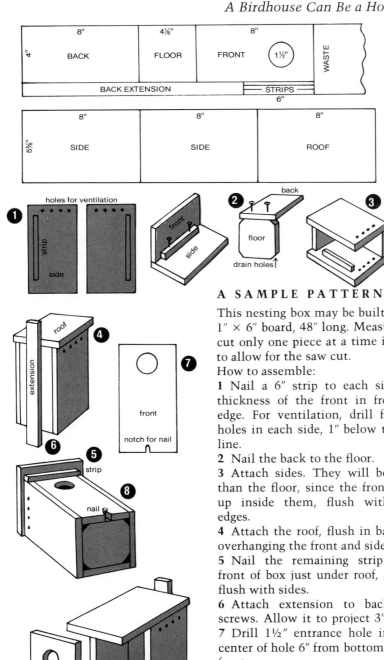

8"	4⅛"	8"			
4" BACK	FLOOR	FRONT (1½")	WASTE		
BACK EXTENSION		STRIPS 6"			

8"	8"	8"
5⅝" SIDE	SIDE	ROOF

A SAMPLE PATTERN

This nesting box may be built from a 1" × 6" board, 48" long. Measure and cut only one piece at a time in order to allow for the saw cut.

How to assemble:

1 Nail a 6" strip to each side, the thickness of the front in from the edge. For ventilation, drill four ¼" holes in each side, 1" below the roof line.

2 Nail the back to the floor.

3 Attach sides. They will be wider than the floor, since the front slides up inside them, flush with their edges.

4 Attach the roof, flush in back and overhanging the front and sides.

5 Nail the remaining strip across front of box just under roof, and cut flush with sides.

6 Attach extension to back with screws. Allow it to project 3" at top.

7 Drill 1½" entrance hole in front, center of hole 6" from bottom edge of front.

8 Cut ⅜" notch in middle of bottom edge, and place on box to mark position of nail. Hammer nail into bottom at top of notch.

House wrens are the easiest species to attract to backyard birdhouses, but entrance holes should be small enough to keep house sparrows from taking over.

THOSE DEPENDABLE, LOVABLE WRENS

The easiest bird to attract to a backyard birdhouse in America is the house wren. This effervescent little fellow is unlike any other birdhouse user in the world. To begin with, the house wren's territory usually consists of your yard and sometimes the adjacent yard or yards. If you put out five wren boxes, the male wren will often build "dummy" nests in all five of them. Later, when the female arrives on the scene, she will select the house she prefers and will then rebuild the nest to her liking. Sometimes she doesn't like any of the sites the male has selected and will seek out her own. Dummy nests are probably decoys to keep predators off balance, as well as a message to other wrens that this territory is occupied.

If you don't put out wren boxes, you might find wrens nesting in your backyard anyway. I have seen them nesting in pumps, knee-

House wrens usually lay 6 or 7 eggs in a nest built of twigs, grasses, plant fibers, rootlets, feathers, hair and rubbish. They normally have 2 broods a summer.

high rubber boots, the radiator of a car, and in both a bathing suit and a pair of overalls hanging on clotheslines.

We hang a wren house from each of the five apple trees in our backyard. The wrens usually select the same box in the same tree year after year, but invariably the other houses are also filled with sticks.

The wrens are perhaps our most welcome summer residents. They arrive in Wisconsin in early May and are well into their nesting activities by late May. Each time we walk the 70 yards to or from the garage, we pass the "wren tree." They are always there, and always have some response to make at our passing by.

DON'T FORGET CHICKADEES AND TITMICE

Most backyard birders forget that chickadees and tufted titmice will nest in birdhouses. A great many feeding stations cater to these winter favorites, but when spring arrives, the proprietors forget that the perky little birds are tree cavity nesters and will use houses.

Chickadees are often overlooked as possible backyard nesters. Darlings of the feeding station, chickadees will nest in birdhouses. Backyard bird watchers interested in keeping chickadees around all year should consider putting up houses with a 1¼-inch entrance hole.

Like chickadees, titmice are also favorites of the feeding station, but are usually forgotten when nesting season arrives. Their houses, requiring a 1⅛-inch entrance hole, should be located high in deep cover.

They like nesting sites in deeper woods than wrens, therefore 4–10 feet high in the deepest cover in your yard is the place to put the houses. The entrance hole is 1⅛ inch for chickadees and 1¼ inch for titmice. If you are successful in getting chickadees or titmice to nest in your yard, it will be something to remember. Not only are the activities of the adults worth monitoring, but when the youngsters fledge, they are the cutest, most lovable balls of cotton you have ever seen.

TREE SWALLOWS ARE WATER BIRDS

If you have a large pool, pond or lake on your property and you live in the northern third of the United States, chances are that you can attract tree swallows to birdhouses. (Violet-green swallows in the West.)

The house is more apt to be used by the green-backed swallows if it is mounted 5–8 feet above the water on the trunk of a dead tree. Tree swallows are nice birds to have around and, if you have the right habitat, you have a good chance to attract them.

Any backyard with a large pond or lake, located in the northern third of the U.S., has a better than even chance of attracting tree swallows to a birdhouse. Place the house on a post near or right over the water for best results.

PURPLE MARTINS ARE FUSSY

Everyone would like to have purple martins in their yard, but martins are fussy. They prefer to be near water and they like to have their houses in open areas, where they can sweep up to the nesting box from a long way off. And, if you don't have any martins in the general proximity of your home to begin with, the chances are not good that you can attract them. I don't mean to be discouraging, only realistic. Most would-be martin houses usually become "ghettos" for house sparrows or starlings. However, if you already have martins in your area, give it a try: you may be lucky. Kit's sister and her family were lucky when they put a martin house on a high post next to their Wisconsin farm pond. Martins from nearby took up residence in the new Dettmer house and multiplied to the point where a second house has now been erected and occupied.

BIG BOXES FOR BIG BIRDS

Screech owls, kestrels (sparrow hawks), flickers and red-bellied woodpeckers will use a birdhouse. The chances of attracting these species to your backyard are less likely, but not impossible. Flickers particularly are common yard nesting species and will give you many hours of entertainment if they select your home as theirs.

NESTING SHELTERS ARE FUN

Robins, phoebes and barn swallows are common backyard species that will use some kinds of shelters but will not nest in a birdhouse. All three use mud and grass to plaster their nests to rafters, crotches of trees or the girders of bridges. A bird shelter with a floor, one or two sides and a roof will suit them fine and, if placed in an area to their liking, may be just what they are looking for.

THE ROOSTING BOX

Welles Bishop manufactures a roosting box. It is a rather large birdhouse with the hole at the bottom, instead of at the top. The

Those backyard bird watchers who are successful in getting flickers to nest around their homes will find they are fun birds, particularly when the young are big enough to stick their heads out of the hole.

During incubation period (only 3 of these eggs were fertile).

Robins will use a shelter or shelf for their nest if it is located in the right place. This series shows the complete life history of one robin family living in western Pennsylvania. Here, the robins build their nest.

Youngsters only a few days old.

Female brooding week-old young.

Fledgling youngsters ready to leave the nest.

idea is that birds will roost in the box, particularly in cold or inclement weather. Inside the box, perches line the sides so that eight to ten birds theoretically can use the roosting box at the same time. We have had our roosting box out for one complete winter and have not seen a single bird use it. Furthermore, on examining the inside, we found no droppings. However, that doesn't mean that it would not work in some yards. The principle makes sense. I suspect that house sparrows are most likely to use the roosting box because of their gregarious nature and habit of getting into similar small places to roost.

NATURAL BIRDHOUSES

Some backyard bird watchers try to keep their yards looking as natural as possible. They use no manmade feeders and no manmade birdhouses. Nonetheless, these people are successful in attracting hole-nesting birds to their yards by bringing in natural nesting cavities. They find fallen trees and stumps with natural cavities and move them to their yards. A dead tree set in concrete in front of the shrubbery border can be a very attractive addition to the backyard

Some backyard bird watchers don't like the looks of artificial birdhouses in their yard but prefer the natural look, such as this dead tree that a downy woodpecker selected for its home in a Pittsburgh area yard. Dead snags like this can be anchored in concrete to create backyard nesting and feeding trees.

Another natural-looking bird-house is a hollow gourd with an entrance hole. Some backyard bird watchers have attracted purple martins to large collections of hanging gourds.

landscape. Not only does it offer nesting sites, but it also makes a natural landing and perching place. By drilling one- or two-inch holes in the trunk, the dead tree will also give you a place for feeding suet. That means that the dead tree is in service all year long.

The use of hollowed-out gourds will also give the backyard a more natural look. We know people who have successfully attracted wrens, tree swallows and purple martins with large numbers of gourds.

PLACEMENT: WHEN AND WHERE

Get the houses out early. Not only will they be there when the birds are ready to use them, but a little weathering on the house doesn't hurt. Refer to the chart for the proper height, color and location. We usually put our birdhouses up as soon as the first flock

Cat and dog hair, yarn and synthetic material are all potential nesting materials. Hang them in an onion bag near the feeders or the watering area where birds will see it and hopefully use it.

of robins crowd into our yard in late March or early April. Farther south, the date is early February.

Give your house-nesting birds, and others, too, a little help with nesting materials. We hang yarn, cotton, hair (our cat, who never goes outdoors, is a welcome donor), straw, loose wool, or synthetic fibers near the feeders where they are easily seen. You will be surprised how many birds will use these materials.

Just as you must maintain the yard furniture and screens, birdhouses must be cleaned and, if necessary, repaired and painted each year. Not only is it a good idea to remove the old nest for hygienic reasons, but an empty box is more likely to attract birds than one full of old nesting material.

Though some of the larger houses, like our wood duck/screech owl box, can be left out all year long, they, too, should be cleaned and maintained at least once a year. It is best to take down all the smaller boxes each fall and put them up again in the early spring. Be careful when storing them in the shed or garage. They make excellent winter homes for mice. By sealing the entrance holes, you can avoid that problem.

The remains of an old bird's nest was placed near a bird house in western Pennsylvania in the hope that a prospective occupant would find nest building easy and convenient.

Birdhouse maintenance is important to the longevity of the house and the nesting success of the birds. Wildlife biologist Dick DeGraaf cleans out a wren house in his backyard in Amherst, Massachusetts, as he prepares to store it for winter.

HOW TO ENJOY YOUR TRIUMPH

If you are successful in "renting" one or more of your backyard birdhouses, make the most of the short period that the birds are in residence. Spend some time watching the birds build. How often do you see the female outside the box when she is incubating eggs? When the eggs hatch, notice that the feeding increases as the young grow. Can you hear the youngsters calling for food?

Most backyard birds are tolerant of humans and you can look into the houses occasionally without disturbing the birds. Use discretion. A good way to look into a nest or nesting box is with a small mirror at the entrance hole. Don't remove the lid or roof unless it can be done easily and without moving the house. If the adults will feed the youngsters while you are standing close to the house, fine. But if they are disturbed by your presence, leave them alone. Most important is to enjoy what you have. After all, that's what backyard bird watching is all about.

Most backyard nesting birds will tolerate humans looking into their house if done discreetly. The use of a mirror to see into the box is better than disturbing it by taking off the roof.

5

The Importance of Water

SURPRISINGLY, WATER is the one basic need that is most often overlooked when setting up a backyard birding habitat.

A LITTLE WATER GOES A LONG WAY

Sufficient water for birds does not necessarily mean an expensive
pool or pond. It can be as simple as an upside-down garbage can lid.

*Water for birds doesn't mean an expensive pool or pond. It can be offered
in as simple a container as an upside-down garbage can lid.*

Surrounded by stones and plants, the garbage can lid can be an extremely popular and attractive spot in your overall setup. At my father's home on Sanibel Island, Florida, wintering red-winged blackbirds, cardinals, robins and ground doves flocked into his yard by the hundreds to bathe in and drink from a garbage can lid which, because of its popularity, needed to be filled hourly. Another Sanibel couple used a large two-inch-deep ceramic pan under their sea grape tree to satisfy the water needs of their birds.

Walter and Barbara Steward of St. John's, Michigan, used a plastic liner two feet in diameter in the depression they had created to hold water. They surrounded the small pool with rocks and plants to make it an attractive setting as well as a useful drinking and bathing area for birds.

Not far to the east, in Clio, Michigan, Marjorie McLaren used plastic liners to build a recirculating triple-decker set of pools. She

The Stewards of St. John's, Michigan, used a plastic liner 2 feet in diameter in a depression they created to hold water for the birds in their backyard.

found that the robins were delighted with the moving water. Surprisingly, deer have been seen drinking at her pool in the middle of a well-developed neighborhood.

BIRD BATH IS THE SIMPLEST

Of course, the most common watering device is the bird bath, which is merely a ceramic or plastic dish on a pedestal. Bird baths work well and certainly are an asset to any yard without water. They work best, however, near cover where birds can quickly escape from predators.

The bird bath need not be placed on a pedestal. My father placed the top of a typical bird bath right on the ground. It was so popular

The most common way to make water available to birds is with a ceramic bird bath on a pedestal. Not only do these bird baths work well, but they are attractive in the backyard setting.

The bird bath in this Sanibel, Florida, yard attracted a rather unusual bather, but red-shouldered hawks need water just as much as robins and cardinals.

that even a red-shouldered hawk used it daily. What a shock to see that big hulk of a bird standing in the middle of the ceramic dish bathing and drinking like any other bird!

Another simple device is a poultry waterer, which is nothing more than a Mason jar turned upside down to release water into a circular trough.

MORE ELABORATE POOLS ENHANCE THE BACKYARD

Some backyard bird watchers have built concrete pools, and some even stocked their pools with goldfish, sunfish and pond lilies. A couple in Hagerstown, Maryland, found that a recirculating waterfall helps aerate the aquatic plants, fish, frogs and snails they have in their patio pool.

Backyard birders in Oak Grove, Louisiana, built a concrete pool

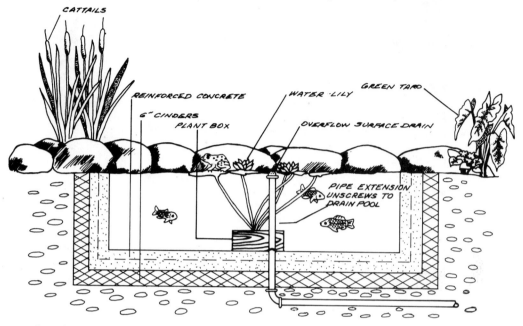

This design, provided by the National Wildlife Federation, is just one of many ways to build your own backyard bird pool.

after the water and fish in its plastic predecessor were washed onto the grass during a heavy rain.

The 12-foot-round concrete pool built by a Walcott, Connecticut man, has a large rock in the center to facilitate birds' drinking and bathing in the 18-inch-deep water. A stick anchored in a coffee can filled with sand will also provide birds with a perch from which to drink in the middle of a deep pool.

SOME OTHER WATER SOLUTIONS

The Robert Vanderpoels of Des Plaines, Illinois, found crater rocks at their local nursery. These stones have natural pockets in them that will hold water. The Vanderpoels have three of four of these rock pools scattered around their grounds. Several are large enough to maintain small fish and a pond lily, and all of them make excellent bird baths.

The Charles Haines family of Fairport, New York, discovered a

Crater rocks purchased at a Des Plaines, Illinois, landscaping firm made interesting and popular waterholes for songbirds in the backyard of the Robert Vanderpoels. They even maintained sunfish and pond lilies in larger rocks.

A seeping spring in the backyard lawn of the Charles Haines residence in Fairport, New York, was planted with cattails to create a miniature marsh for birds.

seep in the back end of their yard. Capitalizing on a good thing, which might be considered by some as a messy area, they planted cattails in the seep and now have a little marsh of about 4 × 8 feet in which birds and other wildlife find water the year around.

The R. H. Rices of The Dalles, Oregon, also had a spring on their property. They built a concrete pool around it so that the birds and other wildlife could use it daily.

Other ways that bird watchers have provided water in their backyards include diverting a small stream, setting out a round aluminum pan placed on cement blocks, filling sunken No. 10 cans or bottom halves of plastic gallon jugs with water, and hanging a gerbil water bottle in a tree.

THE FASCINATION OF MOVING WATER

We have found that moving, dripping or spraying water has an extra attraction for birds. Vern Gwaltney of Tucson, Arizona, created miniature desert water holes in his yard with dripping hoses.

Another inexpensive, but effective, way to make a noise and at-

Dripping water is magic to thirsty birds like this mourning dove in Arizona. The water was allowed to drip ever so slowly, but in sufficient quantities to satisfy many desert species on the grounds of the Arizona Sonoran Desert Museum near Tucson.

The *drip-drip-drip* of this set-up is another effective technique for drawing birds, especially during their spring migrations. Take an ordinary bucket, put a nail hole in the bottom, hang it up over a pan and fill it with water several times during the day.

tract passing birds with water is through the use of a dripping bucket. Punch a nail hole in the bottom of a galvanized bucket (plastic should work, too), making sure that the hole is not so large that the water will escape rapidly. Suspend the bucket over a pan or an upside-down garbage can lid and watch what happens. The sound of the dripping water is amazingly effective in attracting birds to drink and bathe. I have seen this same setup using a garden hose which was turned on just enough to provide a constant drip. This eliminates the need to carry water to the empty bucket. A dripping hose suspended over a pool works well, too.

To show how effective dripping water can be, consider our bird watcher friend in Pennsylvania who told us, with some disgust, that she had two bird baths in her backyard, but all the birds in her area went next door for water. A dripping faucet at the neighbor's house attracted more attention than the two bird baths in her yard.

Another friend living on the west coast of Florida tells about the day the birds descended on her friend's backyard sprinkler like a swarm of locusts. It was spring, and for those birds migrating north from the Caribbean, the Florida peninsula is the first landfall for at least a hundred miles. The weather had been dry and the lawn sprinkler was turned on. "What happened seemed like a miracle," she exclaimed. "Birds suddenly came from everywhere—warblers, thrushes, bobolinks, flickers, painted buntings." She counted twenty-one species in just fifteen minutes.

WATER MAY BE BETTER THAN FOOD

A three-tiered, recirculating pool on the northeast corner of our patio is always a center of much activity, summer and winter. When building the addition on our home (discussed in the Foreword), the pool was planned as an integral part of the patio design. A Little Giant Pump (model 2E-38N) from the Little Giant Pump Company of Oklahoma City, Oklahoma, moves about 100 gallons of water every hour. The pond holds only 55 gallons, so the water is filtered at least once every hour.

Not only is it an attractive addition to our landscape, but the movement and splashing sounds of the waterfalls attract birds all day, every day. At times, we've seen birds lined up waiting to get a position on the upper pool. One day in August, I noticed nine robins

We added this 3-tiered, recirculating pool to our home, one of the most popular birding spots in our yard.

One of the many summer visitors to this watering area is this female rose-breasted grosbeak.

at the water area at one time. On July 11, there were five robins at the pool, four of them juveniles.

During spring and fall migrations, we watch warblers, vireos and thrushes drinking and bathing. During the summer months, we are entertained daily by rose-breasted grosbeaks, goldfinches, robins, catbirds, red-eyed vireos and yellow warblers. We have watched scarlet tanagers, wood thrushes, hermit thrushes, northern (Baltimore) orioles, redstarts, Nashville warblers, brown thrashers and towhees drinking and bathing. During the winter, we see a different parade of birds, including purple finches, redpolls, evening grosbeaks, pine grosbeaks, pine siskins, blue jays, cardinals, chickadees, nathatches and tree sparrows at the water. And then there was the screech owl at the stroke of midnight one New Year's Eve. The pool seems to be every bit as attractive to birds as the food we put out.

OPEN WATER ON A FREEZING DAY

During the winter months in the North, keeping water from freezing becomes a special problem. Small pools and bird baths can be kept free of ice by using a small water heater (available in hardware and lawn and garden centers). Larger pools can be kept open by using cattle trough, or stock tank, heaters (available at farm supply stores).

I never realized how important water in winter was until we installed a cattle trough heater in our pool. We use a 1,000-watt heater that turns on only when the water temperature drops below 40 degrees Fahrenheit (4–5 degrees Celsius). Unfortunately, we had forty-five days in a row last winter when the temperature never got above 32 degrees (zero on the Celsius scale). But it was during that period that our pool was the busiest. We were surprised at how many birds came for a drink on freezing winter days. Not many took baths, but they certainly did drink. It had to be the only open water in our township, perhaps in our county.

A family in Ozawkie, Kansas, had a unique way of providing warm water on subfreezing days. They utilized their backyard gaslight, which was always burning. By placing a garbage can lid upside-down on the top of the lamp, separated from the heat by a circle of galvanized sheet metal eight inches high, they were able to offer the birds warm water all winter long.

Heating the water is the only satisfactory way to keep it from freezing. *Do not use chemicals,* such as antifreeze. They will harm the birds' feathers and destroy their ability to keep warm, not to mention what the chemicals would do internally.

I'm convinced that open water on a freezing winter day will attract as many birds to your yard as food and cover.

Birds bathe and drink at this pool during all 12 months of the year. Open water on a subfreezing day is very attractive and convenient to feeding station visitors. At times the water seems to be more popular than the food.

6

Problems in Eden

SHOW ME a successful backyard bird habitat, and I'll show you an operation that also has problems. It is a proven fact that the same basic needs—food, cover and water—that attract cardinals, chickadees, red-headed woodpeckers and orioles, will also attract house sparrows, starlings, pigeons and grackles, as well as squirrels and chipmunks.

Unfortunately, the backyard bird watcher who has done it all "by the book" will also inevitably have succeeded in creating problems for the desirable species, not to mention himself. What can be done about it?

I wish there was a simple solution, but every backyard is different, and each problem has to be solved separately. Besides, one man's pest is another man's joy.

Nevertheless, there are some things that can be done to discourage the birds and other wildlife you do not want. Generally it amounts to being careful what you feed and how you feed it. Also, there are devices you can use to keep mammals, like squirrels and rabbits, from eating everything in sight. Finally, it is a good idea to use a number of small feeders instead of one large one to ensure a greater distribution of birds. Let's take a look at the most prevalent backyard birding problems and what people have done to solve them.

It is unfortunate that the backyard bird watcher who has created a model area for birds has also created a model area for nuisance wildlife such as gray squirrels, chipmunks, and an assortment of undesirable birds.

PESTS AT THE FEEDERS

There is no doubt in my mind that having too many greedy gray squirrels is the number one feeding station problem all over America. Not only do they consume great quantities of expensive bird food, but they chase the birds away while they are doing it.

The squirrel problem becomes serious for owners of bird feeding stations when a squirrel population explosion occurs. The animals

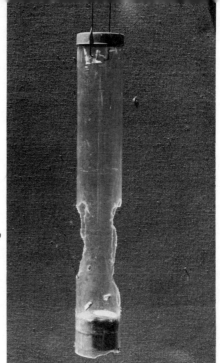

Squirrels will destroy bird feeders to get to the last seed in the bottom.

get so desperate for food that they chew plastic and wooden feeders to get to the last seed. Feeders are expensive and something has to be done.

The squirrel problem is particularly challenging because we are dealing with a clever animal highly skilled in the art of balancing and jumping. I know birders who have spent days, weeks and even months trying to outsmart squirrels and have failed. A couple of examples:

Ed and Jean LeRoy live in a lovely subdivision near Milwaukee. There are lots of trees and many birds to feed in their yard. The LeRoys were excited the day they set out their first bird feeder on a post in the middle of their backyard, but they soon became discouraged when the "cute" gray squirrels emptied their feeder even before the birds had found it.

They had heard about squirrel baffles, so Ed purchased the typical metal disc-type and placed it on the post under the feeder. It stopped the squirrels for only about five minutes. They began jumping to the feeder from a nearby tree. Ed cut the limb. They jumped from the tree trunk. Ed cut down the whole tree. The squirrels began jumping from another tree. No matter where Ed placed the feeder, the squirrels could jump onto it from a nearby tree. The squirrels even learned how to get over the baffle by pulling it down and

There are simple devices that will control squirrels under the right conditions. This squirrel baffle is the most popular and may work if the post feeder is high enough and far enough away from trees to keep the squirrel from jumping.

Sometimes it doesn't work.

crawling over it. Ed built a better baffle that would not bend, but the last we heard, the squirrels were still eating well from the LeRoy pole feeder.

At the Schlitz Audubon Center, also in Milwaukee, the personnel established an experimental bird feeding operation to test seed preferences of various species. They were immediately challenged by gray squirrels who gobbled up all the experimental seed before the birds could get to it. The feeders were suspended on a wire, so the Center people strung coffee cans, 33-rpm records and large beads on the wire, but the agile squirrels mastered all of those obstacles quickly. The next deterrent the Auduboners tried was a large square piece of plastic at each end of the wire, but the squirrels learned to leap over the plastic wall and land skillfully on the coffee cans, beads, etc. That problem, too, remains unsolved.

To show you how persistant squirrels can be, our friends, the Tom Rosts, watched a flying squirrel jump and fall from a feeding station one night forty-six times before hitting the feeder right. It never missed the feeder again. The Rosts then were amazed to note that the squirrel consumed 10 sunflower seeds every minute for the next twenty-five minutes. That's 250 seeds! He was hungry!

Bird feeders are not the only ones having trouble with pesty gray squirrels. The President of the United States has his problems, too. One recent spring, the gray squirrels in Lafayette Square, the President's park, ate two thousand geraniums, girdled and killed over a half dozen newly planted trees and seriously injured some hundred-year-old oaks.

SOME SOLUTIONS

The squirrel baffles will work, but they are not foolproof. When I wrote an article for *National Wildlife* in which I made the statement that the "foolproof" squirrel baffle has yet to be designed, I received dozens of letters challenging that statement. Each letter writer had, indeed, outwitted the squirrels in his backyard with various devices. Most used rigs mounted under the post feeder to keep the squirrel from climbing up the post and onto the feeders. If the post feeder can be placed away from trees and high enough so that the squirrel cannot jump up to it from the ground, the baffle should work. There is also a sliding post that drops to the ground

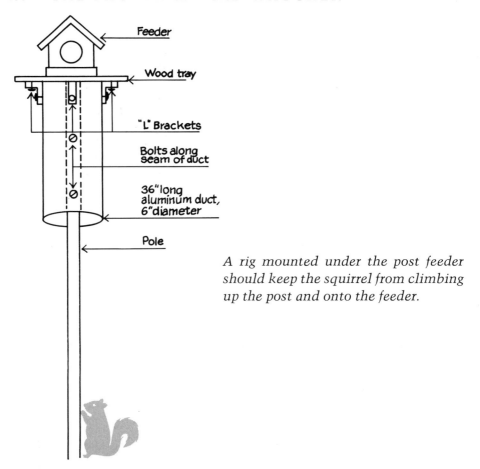

A rig mounted under the post feeder should keep the squirrel from climbing up the post and onto the feeder.

with the weight of the squirrel's body, but most squirrels can outwit that one with some practice.

The most effective solution for the squirrel problem is to get rid of the squirrels. One birder put it this way, "Consider the squirrel a weed in your garden." There are several ways to "get rid" of squirrels. The most humane way is to trap and transfer the animals to some far-off location. Using a Havahart Trap from the Havahart Trap Company, Ossining, New York 10562, you can easily trap squirrels without injuring them. Most people who trap and transfer squirrels transport them in the trap. Be sure to take the animal far enough away so that it will not return—that means at least ten miles.

Another, who is also a hunter, looks upon the squirrels and rabbits in his backyard as a crop of the land to be harvested each fall. That particular family trapped and ate eighteen squirrels the first year, twenty-five the second, and sixteen the third. So far this year, they have harvested twenty-six more. In the rabbit class, they trapped and ate five, four, and three in successive years, and eight so far this year. "We eat them right back," the lady of the household told me when I asked her how much bird food the squirrels eat. If you plan to solve your squirrel or rabbit problem in this manner, be sure to check on the regulations with your local game protector.

Many backyard bird watchers like having squirrels around, and that's fine. My advice to you is to feed the squirrels peanuts and other things in an area where they can find the food easily. Hopefully they will eat at their designated spots and leave the hanging and post feeders to the birds.

One way to get rid of nuisance wildlife is to capture it in a Havahart trap and transport it far enough away so that it will not find its way back to the feeders.

Some backyard bird watchers love squirrels, and that's fine. The best way for them to handle squirrels is to give them their own feeders with the food they like most.

Chipmunks, too, create great problems. Not only do they carry away and store great quantities of bird seed, but they also destroy flowers, vegetables and birds' nests.

CHIPMUNKS ARE CUTE, TOO

Chipmunks often cause the same problems that the gray squirrels do, though they are not as agile at climbing and they hibernate during the coldest months.

Last year, after the chipmunks ate our cultivated strawberries, hoarded hundreds of pounds of bird seed and uprooted the begonias in our patio flower boxes, I decided to start a trap-and-transfer program. The first week I trapped twelve; the next week ten more. By the end of June, I had trapped thirty-five chipmunks and delivered all of them to a lush woodland many miles away and on the other side of an expressway.

Did this solve the problem? No. As I trapped chipmunk after

After trapping and transporting 46 chipmunks from my yard, I still had a chipmunk problem. It was a classic case of a natural vacuum being filled as each animal was removed.

chipmunk, I created a natural vacuum that was immediately filled by other chipmunks from the surrounding area. I did notice that we saw fewer of the little devils, and those that we did see appeared to be less tame.

In October, I trapped five more, and six additional animals this spring, for a total of forty-six to date. But as I write this paragraph in April, I can see three chipmunks on the terrace, one of them loading its cheeks with seed from a feeder.

As stated in the beginning of the chapter, we have done a good job of attracting birds and in the process have also created problems. The chipmunk problem remains unsolved.

HOUSE SPARROWS ARE WELL NAMED

High on the list of pesky birds is the house sparrow, also called the English sparrow, weaver finch and "spatzy," as we called them when I was growing up in Pennsylvania. House sparrows are well

The house sparrow is another major problem at many feeding stations. The best way to discourage them is to avoid feeding cracked corn and baked goods, and to use only hanging feeders that swing in the wind.

named for their affinity for nesting and feeding near people's homes, as well as the fact that they often nest in birdhouses. They used to be even more plentiful in America, but with the loss of the horse as our primary means of transportation, the house sparrow's source of food, horse feed, declined and so did the bird.

The best way to limit the number of house sparrows at your feeders is to use as many hanging feeders as possible. The house sparrow prefers to feed from the ground and at feeders that are well anchored. Another approach that will help, though not eliminate the bird, is to feed as much sunflower seed as possible. House sparrows will eat sunflower, but they much prefer corn and bakery products.

When I was a boy, my dad had a house sparrow trapping project in our backyard. We started the winter with 29 spatzies feasting at our feeders. Over a period of one winter, he trapped and removed 469, but ended up with 35 at the feeders, which was the same problem I had with chipmunks.

Retired Pennsylvania botanist Bill Grimm, now living in Greenville, South Carolina, told me recently that he had destroyed three thousand house sparrows in less than ten years, but he still had them at his feeding station. He told me that he had purchased satellite feeders because they are advertised as being exclusively for chickadees, titmice and nuthatches. House sparrows and the larger perching birds are not supposed to be able to use them. He went on to say that his house sparrows had mastered the use of the satellites and he was upset.

A woman in Dover, Pennsylvania, solved her house sparrow and blue jay problem by placing all of her feeders close to her house. "Chickadees and titmice use them," she told me, "but the sparrows and jays are afraid to come that close to the house."

House sparrows will also invade most birdhouses. Therefore it is worthwhile to use the prescribed entrance hole dimensions and do *not* put a perch on the box. House sparrows prefer perches; most other species do not need one at the entrance.

As I pointed out in the beginning of this chapter, there are no foolproof ways to solve many of these pest problems, but some things do work for some people.

STARLINGS ARE TOUGH TO OUTWIT

Much of what has been said about the house sparrow can be repeated for the starling. Their diet, however, differs somewhat. Those that visit our feeders prefer the suet, almost to the exclusion of every other food. Eating suet, they compete with the hairy, downy and red-bellied woodpeckers and thus are a nuisance.

The best way to discourage starlings at your feeders is to withhold their favorite foods and to place the foods you do feed in hanging feeders. However, you might discourage the woodpeckers in the process. Some people maintain a "nuisance feeder" filled with suet and table scraps to keep the starlings off the woodpecker feeders.

Starlings are even more persistent as nest builders. Pair after pair took up residence in our wood duck and flicker boxes. By destroying one or both of the pair we kept the box empty only for a matter of hours until another pair moved in. The same old "natural vacuum" problem again.

Someone told me I could discourage starlings by putting a mirror on the back wall of birdhouses, opposite the entrance holes, because

Starlings present a different problem at feeding stations. They love suet and can be discouraged if suet is not offered, but then the woodpeckers may disappear too. One backyard bird watcher got rid of her starlings by moving the suet feeder closer to the house where the starlings were afraid to go.

One recommendation for keeping starlings out of bird boxes is to install a mirror on the wall opposite the entrance hole. That scared the starlings at our habitat for only a few minutes until they got used to it.

the starling would see its reflection and be frightened away. That worked for a couple of hours, but our starlings got used to seeing themselves and moved in.

ONE PEST TAKES CARE OF ANOTHER

We had to give up on starlings when we left town for a couple of weeks last spring. When we returned home we found that there already were youngsters in the nesting box. A week or so later, we were sitting on the patio when we heard blood-curdling screams coming from the starling nest. The parents were fluttering at the entrance hole and my first assumption was that the parents were trying to get the young to leave the box. But the more I heard the screams, the more I realized that something was inside the box killing the young. It was interesting to see how many other birds were attracted to the scene and upset by the young starlings' panicky calls. Suddenly there were robins, catbirds, orioles and red-eyed vireos, all sounding alarm notes. We waited and watched and, much to our surprise, the culprit was a chipmunk. It emerged from the box about five minutes after the young stopped shrieking. I did not know that chipmunks were that carnivorous.

JAYS ARE SCOUNDRELS

Speaking of scoundrels, the blue jay is considered by many to be as much a pest as any of the above-mentioned birds and mammals. Personally, we have no problems with them because there are only two pairs in our area and they visit only a couple of times a day. In other backyards, blue jays are more plentiful and dominate the feeders to the point where something has to be done. I recall seeing more than a dozen blue jays at a backyard feeder in Rhinelander, Wisconsin, last winter.

When dealing with the blue jay, you are up against another strong character. It is brash, bold and aggressive. However, it has some traits that are desirable at the feeding station. It is the first bird to give an alarm note when predators appear (it may also be guilty of sounding false alarms just to clear out the feeders for itself). Its eating habits are different, too. I've watched jays fill their gullets

Blue jays can be feeding station bullies, particularly where they live in large numbers. One habitat in Rhinelander, Wisconsin, had dozens of blue jays, but the people there tolerated them. Blue jays can be an asset to feeding stations because they are the first to sound the alarm when hawks or other predators approach.

with sunflower seeds, like a chipmunk fills its pouches, never stopping to open a single sunflower seed. Apparently it flies off to some secret and protected area where it regurgitates the seeds and then cracks each one before eating it.

Unfortunately, blue jays will eat most of the food that is offered at a typical feeding station and you will not get rid of them by feeding selective seeds. They do not eat Niger seeds, however, and an all-Niger feeding station will discourage them, but the all-Niger feeding station will also discourage cardinals and chickadees. One expert suggests grinding sunflower seeds, hulls and all, in a blender to keep the jays from taking so much away so quickly.

THE BLACKBIRD SCOURGE

We are blessed in the North by having to deal with large flocks of blackbirds only during migration periods. Some backyard bird watchers living in the South may have thousands upon thousands, sometimes millions, of blackbirds around their homes all winter. We don't mind the occasional visit of grackles and cowbirds, and we welcome the first visit of the redwings in the spring, but when the blackbirds arrive in huge flocks, it is time to discourage them somehow.

One woman threw firecrackers at them until the large flocks disappeared. She claims that the loud noise didn't discourage her regular visitors. I have found that one or two shotgun blasts into the tree where they are roosting will make them move on. Another way to discourage them at the feeders is not to feed corn or baked goods. They do not like to eat from hanging feeders and will not eat Niger seed. So, selective feeding and removal of feed from the ground should help.

CITY PIGEONS AT CITY FEEDERS

Pigeons plague some feeding stations, though mostly in city areas where these birds are common. The same selective feeding and use of hanging feeders should help to discourage these ground feeders.

SMALL BIRD FEEDERS HELP

Hyde's, Inc., make what they call a Small Bird Feeder that has a wire mesh large enough to admit finches and chickadees, but too small for blue jays and blackbirds. These screened feeders come in both hanging and post assemblies and do an effective job of limiting the larger birds at the feeding station.

Hyde's also manufactures a feeder they call the Tip-Toe. It has a weighted treadle that can be set so only lightweight birds like chickadees and titmice can stand on the treadle without lowering it. When larger birds, like blue jays, land on the treadle, it immediately drops three inches to cover the food with a sheet of metal. When the heavy bird flies away, the treadle rises again so that the lighter-weight birds can feed.

Hyde's Small Bird Feeder, loaded here with pine siskins and goldfinches, will also keep out larger birds. Chickadees are particularly adept at getting through the wire mesh.

Still another style of small bird feeder shows a tufted titmouse at an Easton, Pennsylvania, habitat.

One way to keep blue jays from eating at least some of the food is to use this Hyde's Tip Toe, which has a weighted perch. It can be set so that heavier birds like blue jays, starlings and grackles will lower the perch when they land on it, thus causing a strip of metal to cover the food. Lightweight birds like this yellow-rumped warbler can stand on the perch without moving it and can easily get to the food.

THE MENACE OF SOME MAMMALS

I'd be derelict if I didn't also point out that feeding stations can attract some undesirable mammals like skunks, opossums, raccoons and even rats. Most of these creatures raid the feeders at night, and the best way to get rid of them is by trapping and transferring or destroying. Some people like having raccoons visit them. They even make a nightly ritual in feeding them, some right from the hand. This kind of taming is not in the best interest of the animal or the people. The raccoon can become so tame that it will

Other backyard bird watchers make the mistake of feeding raccoons, skunks, opossums and even bobcats with table scraps. These mammals can create problems that will make well-meaning people wish that they had never started it at all.

There are many ways to store grain for the feeding station, but the challenge is to keep it dry and away from rodents. One possibility is this garbage can setup to store sunflower and wild bird seed mixture.

intimidate the homeowner into feeding it more, and more often. The same is true of squirrels.

Conservation writer Mel Ellis told us about the gray squirrels at his summer cottage in northern Wisconsin. Mel and his wife thought it was nice to have the squirrels feeding from their hands. They even allowed them to enter the kitchen to get their own food from the storage bin. That went on until the Ellises returned to their cottage after being gone for several weeks to find that the squirrels couldn't wait for them. They had chewed their way into the kitchen and had eaten all the food.

PREDATORS HAVE THEIR NEEDS, TOO

Someone once defined a predator as "any creature that beats you to another creature you wanted." Perhaps that applies more to hunters and fishermen, but in some ways it also applies to predators at feeding stations.

It is not unusual to have an American kestrel (sparrow hawk), sharpshin or Cooper's hawk "finchnapping" at feeding stations. It happens at our feeders. I'll never forget the first time a kestrel took one of our juncos. Kit and I were reading in the living room when suddenly every bird at the feeders panicked as if a bomb had exploded. Many hit the windows, others scattered in every direction. A brightly-colored male kestrel swooped down to the patio and grabbed a junco with its talons. The falcon landed in the linden tree and we watched as it skillfully removed the junco's head and then flew away with the remains clutched in its talons. What an experience! It has happened many times since then, but the shock has not been nearly as great as the first time. In fact, after discussing it, we have decided that we approve of the hawk's forays, that it is all a part of nature's way. Of course, we don't like to see our juncos, goldfinches and redpolls taken, but we know that the falcon has a function and has to live, too. There certainly is a surplus of songbirds at our feeders.

Some birders are not so tolerant and take drastic action against such attacks by killing the birds with pole traps or by shooting

One of the most dramatic incidents at our feeders during the production of this book was the day that the male American kestrel (sparrow hawk) picked off a junco from the window feeder.

them. We don't approve of this kind of reaction, particularly in view of the precarious status of most birds of prey. Besides, it is illegal.

The same is true of owls, though most owls are nocturnal and most of their predation is not witnessed by humans.

THE APPEARANCE OF THE SHRIKE

If you live in the North, as we do, you may be visited occasionally by a northern shrike. Southerners see the loggerheads. They are striking black and gray birds that prey on songbirds and insects. When a shrike appears on the scene, the feeding station becomes deserted as it does when a hawk is near. We have never seen a shrike actually take a bird from our feeders, but we have seen them put on a convincing chase.

DOGS AND CATS ON THE PROWL

Neighborhood dogs and cats often interfere with the tranquility of the feeding station routine. I've learned that by opening the door quickly and making a loud bearlike grunt at them, most dogs and cats will hightail it off the property. If you do that often enough, the critter may be too frightened to come on your property.

Another approach is to call the owners and ask that they keep their pets at home. Dogs and cats should not be allowed to run loose, and a gentle reminder to the owner may help. Some people attach bells to their cats to give early warnings to birds.

SUICIDE WINDOWS

Large, clear windows such as those we have overlooking our backyard habitat can create serious problems. Under certain lighting conditions, birds leaving the feeders see the reflection of the trees and sky in the glass and fly into them, sometimes causing injury or death (see chapter 7 for treatment of birds that have hit windows).

Had we known better when we designed our addition, we would have asked the contractor to tilt the glass about five to six degrees downward. That should have eliminated the reflections. However,

Windows that reflect woodland and sky cause problems for birds when they fly into them. There are a number of ways to reduce this problem and ways to help those birds that do hit windows.

we didn't, and we sometimes have fatalities occurring in front of us. My records show that goldfinches are the most vulnerable, followed by juncos. We have also had a mourning warbler, ruby-crowned kinglet, downy woodpecker, red-breasted nuthatch, hermit thrush, Swainson's thrush, purple finch, yellow-bellied sapsucker, redpoll and a belted kingfisher die from a collision with our plate glass windows. That sounds like a lot of dead birds, but compared to those that hit the windows and survived, it is not.

There are a number of ways to keep the birds from flying into the glass if you can't tilt it down. One is to hang colored streamers of cloth or plastic on the outside of the glass. These strips will move in the breeze and discourage birds from flying into them and the glass.

Dr. Harold D. Mahan, Director of the Cleveland Museum of Natural History, designed what he calls an "Owl-ouette," which is an attractive silhouette of a great horned owl that is affixed to the inside of the window. The product, which is copyrighted by the museum, supposedly reduces bird casualties caused by windows by fifty percent. It can be obtained by sending $2.00 to The Cleveland

Museum of Natural History, Cleveland, Ohio 44106. We tried it on our worst casualty window and it seemed to reduce both incidents of collision and fatalities.

McCormick Place in Chicago, the huge exposition center which has enormous glass walls, uses hawk silhouettes to discourage window casualties. Other methods include soaping the glass, placing branches for perching across the outside of the glass and closing the drapes when the reflections are greatest.

If all this fails, don't feel too badly about the victims. Keep in mind that only a small percentage of all songbirds survive their first year, and the few that die against your windows probably would have been killed in another way.

The "Owl-ouette" designed by the Cleveland Museum of Natural History is effective in reducing bird window collisions. See text for details on how to obtain and use it.

YOU CAN'T TAKE THE BIRDS TO FLORIDA

Many backyard bird watchers are concerned about leaving town during winter months when the birds seem to be most dependent on the feeders. The best way to keep from losing your birds is to involve your neighbors in feeding them. When you leave, the birds merely feed in the neighbor's yard until you get home. We have neighbors on both sides of us who feed birds, and it is a matter of only a few hours after we return home that our birds are back. On a recent trip out of the country, we left twenty-five redpolls depending on us for Niger seed. When we returned home two weeks later, we filled the feeders immediately and the redpolls were back in a few minutes. They had spent the two weeks three doors away.

Research into this subject shows that even if you don't have neighbors to take up the feeding slack while you are away, the birds will not starve. They will revert to their ways of gleaning wild food. You will find, however, that it will take much longer to get them back to your feeders if they have reverted back to wild food.

You can't take the redpolls with you to Florida for 2 weeks, but there are ways to keep them and other birds happy while you are away.

If you think you have problems with pest wildlife in your yard, take the case of nature photographers Kent and Donna Dannen of Estes Park, Colorado. They have 1,000-lb. elk browsing in their yard chasing their evening grosbeaks and destroying their bird feeders. When I found humor in this problem the Dannens responded with, "May you awaken tomorrow to find a 1,000-lb. squirrel looking in your window with bits and pieces of your feeders hanging from its whiskers."

PLAYING GOD IS HUMAN

Throughout this section on problems, you will notice that I have been "playing God." "Remove house sparrows and starlings." "Feed selectively for the pretty birds." "Don't blame the kestrel, he has to eat, too." "Don't feel badly about killing a couple of birds on your window; they probably would have been killed anyway." All of these pronouncements sound as though I am setting myself up as God, deciding which are the privileged critters and which have to go.

To justify this, we have to ask ourselves why we are feeding birds to begin with. Certainly not because they will starve if we don't.

The answer is because we enjoy it and because we want to be closer to nature. If we can't enjoy having a backyard bird habitat and if it becomes a chore or hassle, then we would be better off not having birds in our backyards at all. Therefore, I can rationalize my decision on what birds and animals I want in my backyard and which ones I want to keep out, just as I decide what plants I want growing in my garden. But when it's all said and done, none of us are really very successful at playing God, either in our gardens or at our feeding stations—to wit, my war on chipmunks!

7

Traumas of the Backyard Hospital

WHAT DO you do when your ten-year-old comes in the house with tears in her eyes and a bleeding baby downy woodpecker in her hands? Or when the family English setter places a fledgling cardinal

What do you do when your 10-year-old daughter brings in a bleeding downy woodpecker? There are very specific things that you can and should do for the well-being of the bird and the child.

223

at your feet, a bit wet but unharmed? What about the day you mowed the back 40 and ran over a meadowlark's nest, tearing it up and decapitating two of its occupants?

Because it is human nature to want to save a bird that is doomed, and because wildlife is frequently injured, ill or thought to be orphaned, these problems do come up frequently for backyard bird watchers. Too often, we get emotionally involved and make the wrong decisions.

Here are some basics that should be considered when you find an injured or orphaned animal:

It is illegal for any unlicensed person to keep protected wildlife in captivity. All birds except starlings and house sparrows are protected by federal law, and mammals by state law.

From a biological standpoint, captive wildlife is not saved unless it can be returned to the wild to reproduce.

Many injured or orphaned birds wind up in a cardboard box that becomes their coffin after a slow and miserable death. Most people are incapable of caring for wildlife youngsters and should call the proper authorities.

Wildlife that is in captivity for more than a few days can become dependent on humans and therefore should be acclimated to the wild before being released.

Among common species, such as robins and meadowlarks, the reproductive capacity is so great that the population can suffer huge losses without hurting the species in general.

"Orphaned" wildlife—those youngsters that are healthy and have no problems except that their parents are not in sight—should be left right where they are.

The cardinal fetched by the setter should have been released immediately. Its parents would probably respond to its calls. If a young bird has fallen out of a nest, try to put it back; the adults will accept it. Handling a baby bird will not cause its parents to abandon or kill it, as some people believe. If the whole nest has fallen out of the tree, try to put it back and then forget it.

In the case of the mowed-over meadowlarks, the decision should have been to remove the dead, reshape the nest and leave it alone. The female meadowlark would probably return to the nest. The chances for survival of the young are better in the nest, particularly if the youngsters can call. The odds are against humans raising most baby birds successfully.

TO SAVE OR NOT TO SAVE?

Injured birds present a different situation. Turning your back on a blue jay with a broken leg is not easy, though it may be the best decision in the long run. Even if the blue jay does not survive, it could make a meal for a hawk or fox. But most people want to do something—right or wrong, they want to do something. In that case, the best thing to do with the blue jay or the bleeding downy in the hands of your ten-year-old is to call your local conservation officer (state game warden). If the warden is not available, call the Humane Society, SPCA or Audubon Society. These groups are accustomed to such problems and will be helpful. In many large cities there are teams of volunteers who handle such cases. In one metropolitan area, such a group works in cooperation with the Izaak Walton League. The Bird Care and Rehabilitation Program, as it is called, has one person who specializes in caring for birds of prey, another in songbirds and small mammals, while another volunteer

At one time or another, most people must face the question, "Should I save this bird or destroy it?" Knowing what to do and how to do it is important, but don't sentence yourself and the injured bird to weeks of useless care.

This Canada goose was injured at the Horicon National Wildlife Refuge in east-central Wisconsin. It was delivered to the Refuge headquarters, where it received proper and legal care.

merely goes around and picks up the animals and delivers them to the correct clinic. All of these people have state permits to keep wildlife in captivity.

When it is obvious that the animal will not survive, you have to decide whether to allow it to suffer or to destroy it.

Birds with broken limbs should be taken to one of the agencies mentioned above for care and treatment. Don't attempt to doctor a bird yourself. Even if you are successful in splinting the leg or tying the broken wing, its recovery will require a long period of care and feeding. Most people are not qualified to give such care, and the bird usually dies.

TREATMENT OF WINDOW COLLISIONS

It is not uncommon for birds to fly into windows. Apparently they see the reflection of sky or trees in the glass and fly into it (see chapter 6 for ways to prevent bird collisions with windows). When this happens, birds may be either stunned or injured, but a high percentage of those that hit our windows merely fly to the nearest tree, sit there for a few seconds to clear their heads and then go about their business. Of those that do fall to the ground, most are only stunned, not injured. My guess is that only one out of fifty birds that hits our windows dies, and only one out of ten that falls to the ground dies.

Most birds that hit windows and survive the first few minutes will make a complete recovery if handled quickly and properly.

We have discovered that if the bird falls to the ground, but does not die immediately, its chances for a complete recovery are good. To enhance those chances, we put the groggy bird under a large, upside-down kitchen sieve. This is to protect it against predators. If the weather is cold, we bring the bird inside and put it under the sieve on a piece of newspaper. Some people put them in dark, quiet places. Though we keep an eye on the bird, it usually takes from fifteen minutes to two hours for it to recover totally. If it begins to chip or move around, it is ready to be released. It is better to keep the stunned bird under the sieve too long than not long enough.

We have followed this procedure many times and it almost always succeeded. I can remember only one time when a stunned bird didn't recover in a matter of an hour or so. That was the case of "Lady," the female downy woodpecker. Lady hit the window on Sunday, June 12. We put her under the sieve, but she kept her head under her wing all day Sunday and Sunday night. It wasn't until Monday morning that she chipped a little. In spite of her sleepy condition, we decided to put her out on the suet tree late Monday morning. She stayed there all day Monday, and on Tuesday morning we were delighted to see her eating the suet. Lady remained on the suet tree all day Tuesday and Wednesday. When other downies arrived at the tree to feed, she was submissive and allowed the healthier birds to eat first. On Wednesday she became more active and hopped from one branch to another. On Thursday morning she was gone. But around noon we saw her again, hopping across the patio to the suet tree and up the trunk to the food. Later that day, we saw her fly for the first time from the suet tree to the tree next to it. By Friday she was much recovered and was actually chasing other downies away from the suet.

We think we have seen Lady many times since then, though all female downies do look alike. In any event, we believe that we did as much for this bird as anyone should do. We are convinced that care or treatment by untrained people beyond this point is useless and may do more harm than good.

ORPHANS: LEAVE THEM ALONE

For some unexplained reason, many people assume that if a bird is sitting on the lawn or in a tree by itself, it is an orphan and is

When it is cold outside, window victims are brought indoors and placed under a sieve for a couple of hours to recover before being released. This chickadee (and many like it) recovered within 15 minutes to 2 hours and then was released.

Lady, the female downy, was the exception to the rule. It took her days to recover from her collision with the window, though she was released the day after it happened.

Thousands of baby robins are or-phaned by well-meaning people who think the bird's parents have aban-doned it. The best rule when con-fronted by a lonesome-looking baby bird is to leave it alone.

doomed to die unless taken care of. The truth is that the bird only becomes an orphan when that human removes it from its environment. In some cases, the parent bird does not want to show itself because that is one of nature's ways of protecting young wildlife. When danger is present, the adults will often appear only when the young bird sounds an alarm. In other species, such as the killdeer, the parent bird will feign a broken wing purposely to attract attention away from the young.

With this in mind, the rule for all would-be orphans is *leave them alone.* Their chances for survival are far, far greater in their own environment than in the bottom of a dark cardboard box where they get the wrong kind of care and food.

WHAT TO DO WITH A BANDED BIRD

If you find a dead or injured bird marked with a small metal or plastic ring on its leg, you can contribute greatly to our knowledge of the life histories of birds. The bird was probably banded by an official bird bander licensed by both the state and the U.S. Fish and Wildlife Service.

Send the following information about the banded bird to the Migratory Bird Research Laboratory, U.S. Fish and Wildlife Service, Laurel, Maryland 20811: (1) Your name and address; (2) All numbers

You can make a great contribution to the field of ornithology by reporting all banded birds to the U.S. Fish and Wildlife Service. See text for details.

and letters on the band; (3) Date you found it; (4) Where you found the bird (distance and location from nearest town, the county and state); and (5) How you found the bird and its condition.

If the bird is dead, you should remove the band from the bird and send it in with the report. Under no circumstances, however, should you remove the band from a living bird.

Upon receipt of the information, the Fish and Wildlife Service will send your report to the person who banded the bird. The Service will also report back to you on when and where the bird was banded. This information will tell you how far the bird has traveled and how long it has lived since the day it was banded. This kind of banding information has shown that some species of ducks live nearly twenty years, and some species of ocean birds travel many thousands of miles each year.

8

The Art of Backyard Bird Photography

ANY SIGHT in nature worth seeing is worth photographing. After all, photography is nothing more than a permanent record of a sight worth preserving.

We read in nature magazines and books about how top professional bird photographers sit in blinds for hours, sometimes days and weeks, to get perfect bird photographs under perfect conditions. If you consider our homes as blinds—and they are—then we back-

The backyard feeding station is a perfect setup for bird photography. The natural habitat, feeders, birdhouses, water areas and relatively tame birds add up to a great opportunity for good pictures.

Most successful nature photographers spend many hours in blinds await-ing the right moment for perfect photographs. The backyard bird watcher, on the other hand, can wait in comfortable living conditions for the right moment to take photographs through his patio or kitchen windows.

yard bird watchers have an even better opportunity to shoot good bird photographs under ideal conditions. We, too, can wait for days, weeks or even longer if necessary, by merely leaving our cameras set up and going about our daily routine while we wait. We don't have to endure the hardships of cramped, hot (or cold) portable blinds. We can take photographs right through our windows. In addition, our birds are tamer, more abundant and more relaxed than those in the wild.

My son Peter demonstrates the technique of backyard nature photography as a gray squirrel poses. If you consider your house a blind and the wildlife that visits your feeding station as subjects, the opportunities for photography are endless.

In other words, the backyard birding habitat is an excellent setup for bird photography. We have lots of natural habitat for backgrounds, feeders to get the subjects in close, birdhouses and nests to record their domestic lives, water to show them in interesting and sometimes comical poses, and glass windows through which we can record all of it on film.

EQUIPMENT ISN'T THE ANSWER

The secret to taking good nature photographs is not expensive equipment, as many people believe. It is more likely to be the technique and timing used to capture on film those split-second dramas such as pine siskins fighting over food, a chickadee showing its youngsters how to eat suet, a red-shouldered hawk taking a dip in a bird bath and the male cardinal passing a sunflower seed to his mate.

I began taking bird photographs with a 4 × 5 Speed Graphic when I was seven years old. Since then, as I have filmed wildlife in more than forty countries on five continents, I have felt that my knowledge of the wildlife and the way I acted in its presence has been far more important to my success as a photographer than the kind of camera I used. Backyard bird watchers have the advantage of getting to know their subjects well. They know what to expect as each species feeds and, therefore, they can anticipate good photographs as the dramas unfold. For that reason, I am convinced that nearly any backyard bird watcher with any kind of camera—even a $30 Instamatic—can make very respectable bird photographs.

KNOW YOUR CAMERA

Even if you have a very simple camera, know how it works and what it can and cannot do. That way, you can concentrate on the subject, not the mechanical operation of the camera. Practicing the camera is just as important as practicing the piano. When you no longer have to think about how the camera works, you will take better photographs. All of this information applies to movie cameras as well as still cameras.

The art of bird photography has come a long way since 1900, when this Kodak Brownie was made. With the modern Brownie called the Instamatic, backyard bird watchers can make excellent photographs of the birds at feeders. Knowledge of the subject is more important than the equipment being used.

THINK BEFORE YOU SHOOT

Before you push the button, stop and think about some of the basics of good photography:

• *Background*—Does the background look natural or is there a garbage can in it? Does the background show off the subject, or is it so busy that the subject is lost in it? If the background is not right, move the camera a little to the left or right, up or down. Blue sky often makes a good background.

• *Light*—Bright sunlight is often the best illumination for backyard bird photographs. The best times of the day for sunlight photographs are early morning and late afternoon, when the sun is at a low angle and the quality of light is good. High-noon sunlight is colorless and the high angle causes offensive shadows. Keep in mind that it is best to have the sun behind the camera. It is fine to have some sidelighting, but do not shoot right into the sun. That will give you black-looking birds, even if they are goldfinches.

If your feeders are on the north side of the house, the sun may be hidden behind the house during most of the winter months and

Lighting is important. Before you shoot the photograph, check which way the sun is hitting the subject. If the lighting is from the side or from behind the camera, the photograph should be good. Lighting coming right into the camera from the front will make even a yellow goldfinch appear to be black.

your subjects will be in shade. We solved that problem by moving some of our feeders to the east side of the house during winter months.

• *Camera angle*—What is the angle of the camera in relationship to the subject? Is it too high? Too low? Too close? Too far away? Eye level is usually the best camera angle, but sometimes the background will dictate this.

• *Depth of field and shutter speed*—Most bird photographs require fast shutter speeds to stop movement. Depending on the sensitivity of your film, this usually means that the lens aperture must be at a rather wide opening, reducing the depth of field (the area of sharpness). Therefore, it is wise to shoot your photographs at the slowest shutter speed possible (but fast enough to stop any movement), in order to reduce the aperture opening and gain the greatest depth of field. If your camera has preset exposures, you do not have to worry about this.

• *Focus*—Is the lens focused? If part of your subject is closer to the camera than other parts, focus on the closest part, because the depth of field is shallower in front of the subject than behind it.

• *Use of a tripod*—If you own a tripod, use it as often as possible. One of the greatest problems photographers have is holding their cameras still. You can eliminate camera movement by placing it on a tripod.

SHOOT THROUGH GLASS

Many people are afraid to take photographs through glass windows. Don't be. It's easy. Nearly every feeder photograph in this book was shot through window glass. Here are some tips on how to do it:

The room from which you are shooting photographs should be as dark as possible to minimize reflection on the glass as well as movements that could startle the birds.

The better the quality of the glass, the fewer distortions in your photographs. Thermopane glass does not adversely affect photographs.

Try to shoot your photographs straight through the glass. Shooting through glass at an angle increases the distortion.

Many of the photographs in this book were taken through the glass windows in my living room. Using a 400mm Leica lens on a Leicaflex body, I recorded birds at feeders, in birdhouses and bathing in the patio bird pond.

If you are using flash, hold the flash flat against the glass to prevent any reflective bounce-back.

Clean windows give you clearer photographs.

Obviously, a telephoto lens will allow you to get a larger image of the birds you are photographing, but if your feeder is close to the window, a telephoto lens is not necessary. With a little patience, you should be able to train your birds to feed close to your windows, and your camera.

I used a 400mm telephoto lens to record many such bathing scenes at the patio bird pool.

Recovering from a collision with a patio window, this robin was easily approached within a few feet for photographs while it regained its equilibrium.

KNOW YOUR SUBJECTS

Study the birds you intend to photograph. Do they move rapidly? Do they ever stop eating to look around? Do they look at you? What time of the day do they feed? How do they eat? Which is their favorite feeder? Knowing the answers to these questions will help you take better photographs.

USE A DUMMY CAMERA

If you do not want to leave your camera set up at the window all the time, you might consider the use of a dummy camera to get the birds used to having something shiny at the window. The dummy camera can be a No. 10 can on a tripod or stick, or you could nail together a box the size of your camera and paint it silver and black. You will find that the use of a dummy camera will make the birds less afraid of the real thing when it comes time to take pictures. The dummy camera works just as well outside at the wren house or robin nest.

By setting up a dummy camera in the window or backyard near the subject to be photographed, birds will get used to seeing the camera. When the real camera is in place, the birds will be less frightened of it.

MOVE OUT INTO THE BACKYARD FOR PHOTOGRAPHS

Some photographers have setups around their yards with permanent blinds to hide in. Bill Dyer of Lake Wales, Florida, spends many days each June at his Michigan summer home photographing warblers. He has installed a fine spray of water surrounded by lovely mosses and foliage for a perfect photographic setting. Using a long telephoto lens from a blind, Bill has recorded some of the finest warbler photographs I've seen.

Bird photographer Bill Dyer of Lake Wales, Florida, spends the month of June photographing warblers at his summer home in Michigan. This pool of water attracted hundreds of birds to Bill's camera setup.

A black-and-white warbler is just one of many Bill Dyer has photographed at his Michigan water pool setup. From a blind, Bill uses a telephoto lens to make some of the world's finest warbler photographs.

OUR PHOTOGRAPHIC SETUP

Because this book has so many photographs in it, the reader might be interested in the kinds of cameras and films we used. Our workhorses are 35mm Leicaflex cameras. We have two camera bodies and four lenses: 35mm, 60mm (macro), 135mm and 400mm. A few of the photographs were made with an Olympus OM-2 camera, which we are testing. Almost every photograph was made with the aid of a Tiltall tripod. The flash shots were illuminated with either a Honeywell Strobinar 800 or a Vivitar 102. We used Kodachrome 25 and 64 color film and Kodak Plus-X black-and-white film.

WHAT KINDS OF FILM DO YOU NEED?

The kind of film you select will depend on what you want to do with the photographs. If you want prints, use black-and-white film or a color print film. If you want slides, then select color transparency (slide) films. Twelve years of experience on the staff of *National Wildlife/International Wildlife* has told me that Kodachrome 25 or 64 are the best color slide films in the world. They are better than Kodak's Ektachrome because Kodachrome has less grain (the sandy look) in the film and, when enlarged, the photographs look better.

WHAT YOU CAN DO WITH YOUR BIRD PHOTOGRAPHS

There are many uses for good bird photographs. Magazines are always looking for high quality nature photographs and, if you are successful, I would suggest that you contact the photo editors of these publications and show them your work.

I know quite a few backyard bird watchers who have assembled an entertaining slide program for showing at service clubs, schools and family gatherings. Not only are they entertaining, but they are educational and often encourage other people to become backyard bird watchers.

Other photographers we know use their best bird photographs on their Christmas cards, personal stationery or for framing in their

Pretty bird photographs make nice Christmas cards. My father selected this nesting blue jay photograph for his holiday greeting.

homes. Still others enter their best work in local and national photo contests. Some even exhibit their work and sell mounted and framed bird photographs. One backyard bird watcher glues a photograph next to the listing of each species in her record book.

There is no end to the uses you can make of good bird photographs. Try taking some through your kitchen or patio windows.

9

A Calendar for Your Birding Year

BIRDS, LIKE people, live by a calendar. The birds' calendar is a built-in mechanism for behavior, dictated by the relative position of the sun to the earth. Actually, all life on earth is influenced by the sun, but birds seem to respond to its changing positions in a more dra-

The appearance of the first red-winged blackbird at my feeders in late March signals the coming of spring on the birding calendar.

matic way. The birds' calendar is so accurate that a backyard bird watcher can pretty well guess what month it is by looking at the birds in the backyard. Sometimes you can even tell if it is early or late in a particular month by the kinds and appearances of birds that are present. If I saw a male red-winged blackbird and a male goldfinch with blotchy yellow plumage at our Wisconsin feeders, I'd know that it was late March or very early April. If I saw a magnolia or blackpoll warbler in nonbreeding plumage in Wisconsin, I'd know it was September.

Birds are weather prognosticators, too. They are sensitive to pressure changes in the atmosphere and can anticipate storms. If we see our birds feeding more heavily than usual, we know that the storm gods are likely to descend on us. On warm, clear days they feed less heavily.

The arrival of the breeding season also influences the activities of birds. As the breeding season comes on in May, most birds establish their own breeding territories. Those that claim our yard as their nesting area chase away others of the same species. In some cases, the feeding station and the pond are common grounds where all birds of certain species, like robins and goldfinches, are permitted to visit.

It can therefore be said that the birds in our backyards are all living on a predetermined, but ever-changing schedule, affected by the seasons, temperature, weather and their instincts to breed, migrate and defend territories, all of which is dictated by the position of the sun.

Because we know this, we can predict with some certainty that during the month of January, for example, certain species of birds will be at feeding stations in specific parts of the country, and that backyard bird watchers can do certain things to ensure maximum use of their backyards by the birds in their area. With this in mind, we have set up a Birding Calendar in this chapter to help you develop and maintain your backyard as an ideal place to see birds throughout the year. By following the suggestions in this chapter on a month-to-month basis, you stand a better chance of attracting more birds to your yard.

Note: Because we live in southeastern Wisconsin, much of the information in this calendar applies more directly to backyard bird watchers living in northern areas, where snow and freezing temperatures influence birds and bird feeding. Backyard bird watchers living in the South or Southwest can make use of this calendar by adapting it to their own climates.

JANUARY

Deep winter in the North is the peak of the backyard bird feeding year. Snow is usually deep, and one low pressure system after another brings more and more snow. The deeper the snow, the harder it is for birds to find food in the wild, making your feeding station even more inviting.

The feeding station should be in full operation, offering a variety of seeds spread out among a number of feeders. If you haven't tried feeding Niger seed to the finches, you are missing the best of the

January: Brush the snow off feeders after each storm so that hungry birds can find food.

wild bird foods. Beef suet is also important and popular at this time of the year, when birds need this kind of high energy food to keep warm.

If you can keep your bird bath or water pool unfrozen by using a heater, you will discover that open water on a subfreezing day is another surefire bird attraction.

January is also a time for Canadian species like evening grosbeaks, redpolls, pine siskins and crossbills. They love sunflower seeds and a good supply at your feeders could entice them.

In spite of the ice and snow, those who look can find signs of spring. If you have goldfinches, look closely at them. Do they look a little brighter? January is the month when the males show the first signs of turning yellow. Another sign of spring in January is the calling of owls. The great horned owl, in particular, can be heard on clear January nights, even when the temperature is below zero.

This is also a good month to make your yard plan for the trees, plants and other habitat improvements you want to make in your yard this spring. Consider adding some new fruit or seedbearing shrubs, an additional brush pile or more evergreens to provide cover.

And don't get rid of that Christmas tree. Stand it in the corner of the yard or tie it to a fence or another tree. It will give your birds excellent cover at least through spring.

January Checklist:

Fill feeders daily, preferably in late afternoon
Brush snow off the feeders during and after storms
Feed suet for quick energy
Spread out and vary the height of feeders so that more birds can use them
Keep water open on freezing days; it's irresistible
Check goldfinches for color changes—a sure sign of spring
Listen for owls hooting, another sign of spring
Plan for spring plantings

FEBRUARY

Though there are some very early signs of spring, February is still deep winter in the northern United States and a time for maximum use of the bird feeders by winter residents and northern visitors.

February: My daughter Jennie replenishes seeds for ground-feeding birds following a Wisconsin snowstorm.

The feeding station should be used heavily, particularly as low pressure systems approach with more snow and ice. Feeders should be filled daily and the snow and ice brushed off to allow the birds to reach the food.

Evening grosbeaks, redpolls, pine siskins and crossbills are likely candidates to supplement the chickadees, titmice, goldfinches, cardinals, juncos, blue jays, tree sparrows and an assortment of woodpeckers that normally feed in your yard during the winter. Keep a good supply of sunflower seed in at least one feeder for those northern seed eaters.

Niger seed should keep finches happy. Though expensive, Niger seed is well worth the cost.

Suet, usually free from your local butcher, is a necessary winter high energy food. Woodpeckers in particular eat suet throughout a winter day. Downies, hairies, red-bellied and red-headed woodpeckers frequent the suet bag hourly.

Look for more obvious signs of spring in February. Owls can be heard hooting on clear February nights and tree buds are swelling. The great horned owl actually nests in late February. Red-winged blackbirds start arriving in the North.

If you haven't completed your plans for spring planting and backyard habitat improvements, February is a good month for that. Consider the vegetation you have growing already and what you might plant in the spring to make your yard more attractive to birds. Food and cover plants are the key, and if you can find plants that offer both, all the better.

It's time to think about birdhouses and shelters you will put out in the spring. Are they in good repair? Do they need a fresh coat of paint or stain? Do you need to buy or build some new ones?

February Checklist:

    Fill feeders daily
    Keep feeders free of ice and snow
    Provide suet for quick energy
    Keep water open for thirsty birds
    Paint and repair birdhouses and shelters
    Finish plan for spring planting
    Listen for owls hooting
    Look for other signs of spring—goldfinches changing color; buds
       swelling

March: The time to put up birdhouses and shelters.

MARCH

March is the month of awakening, subtly at first, but as the days become noticeably longer, winter begins to lose its grip on the land.

Bird food in the wild is now more scarce than at any other time. Most, if not all, of the seeds and fruits from last summer are either eaten or decomposed. For this reason, birds are responding more to the food available at feeding stations. It is during this month that the redpolls are most abundant. Many a March morning was met at our house with between fifty and one hundred redpolls flitting around the Niger and sunflower seed feeders. Those on the feeders were quarreling over their positions. Those on the ground were reclaiming the black gold that was dropped from the Niger seed feeders. When a hawk threatens, there is an explosion of wings as all those on the ground fly up into the linden trees. Those on the prime perches at the feeders are more reluctant to fly and give up their hard-won positions.

Because of the voracious appetites of winter birds, the feeders should be tended daily, making sure there are several containing each kind of seed to allow more birds to feed at the same time. I have found that by filling the feeders at dusk, the birds will find full feeders at first light the next morning and I don't feel guilty about not rising at the crack of dawn to feed them.

Suet is also important during these last very cold weeks.

Goldfinch males continue to gain a brighter yellow color as the winter wears on. By mid-March we look for the first male red-winged blackbird; others look for the first robin. By late March phoebes and flickers are being seen in the North. We also begin to see chipmunks for the first time since November. Red squirrels are fighting with the grays for food on the ground, and mourning doves have paired off. And who can overlook "Big Red," who has suddenly started his serenade?

By late March you should have your birdhouses up, particularly if you live below the snow belt. By late March spring is coming on strong in the South, and the birds there are serious about nesting.

Southerners should also begin yard work, plantings and any new landscape designs they have in mind.

Depending on where you live, March is the month to hear the first spring peepers. On our lake, the first chorus is heard three days after the ice goes out. That can occur anytime from March 26 to April 22.

So, March is a mixture of late winter and early spring. There are days in the North when fresh, ankle-deep snow and Canadian birds at the feeders make one wonder if spring will ever come. But then there are other days when the temperatures climb well above freezing and the birds begin to tune up their songs and behave like the nesting season is only a few weeks away.

March Checklist:

Fill feeders daily—natural food is in shortest supply
Suet is needed for quick energy
Open water on subfreezing days will be popular
Goldfinch males are turning yellow
Watch for the first male red-winged blackbird, the first robin, phoebe, flicker, tree swallow and chipmunk
Listen for the first spring peeper; the cardinal's song
Southerners, put up birdhouses and start planting and yard work
Northerners, make final plans for spring yard work

APRIL

You know it is spring in April. You can smell it and hear it. It's everywhere.

April is the transition month. In the North, it can be a very snowy, cold season and a critical period for bird feeding.

April is the month that the northern invaders start to return to their Canadian haunts. It is also the time for the first wave of summer residents to return from the South. Every transient species, from Canada geese to hummingbirds, is on the wing. The direction is *north.*

In addition to the regular seeds and suet, April is a good time to add some new foods for those that do not eat seed. Try fruit for warblers, orioles and thrushes. Robins, mockingbirds and wrens like raisins. Crushed nutmeats might interest other migrants.

The water area will be a highlight for migrants. Remember that running or dripping water is far more interesting to birds than still water. In late April we have seen five different species of warblers at our water area at one time.

It was also on a day in late April that we had an invasion of swallows over the lake. There were hundreds of them—barn, tree,

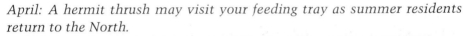

April: A hermit thrush may visit your feeding tray as summer residents return to the North.

rough-winged and bank swallows. Wave after wave would swarm over the now open lake in search of newly hatched insects.

Our loon appears in April shortly after ice-out. Many other kinds of waterfowl appear. One year we counted fourteen species. If you are going to house a wood duck family, this is the month it will happen. Get the house up early.

April is the time to put out all the birdhouses. It's also yard time—a time to clean up from the winter, plant for the summer and begin those landscape projects that were planned in January.

You might also try putting out some nesting materials for those species that like to use yarn, cotton, cat hair or string in their nests.

Early April in the North is as different from late April as winter is from summer, and it is a great month to be a backyard bird watcher. So much is happening from one day to the next that you need a scorecard to know the players.

April Checklist:

Keep feeders full—early April can be as wintry as January
Suet is important on those cold days
Migrants are attracted to running water like bears to honey
Say goodbye to the Canadian invaders, hello to the first summer residents
Note the absence of juncos and tree sparrows
Put up birdhouses
Hang nesting materials from limbs and fence posts
Clean up and start planting
Make lists of birds seen in April—it may be the biggest month for numbers

MAY

The merry month of May is one of the most rewarding for the backyard bird watcher. It is a month when all the summer residents return to your backyard, full of song and enthusiasm. It is a month when your feeders and water area are visited by new species, never before seen in your yard, and perhaps never again.

To keep the feeders busy, a greater variety of food is needed. Reduce the number of seed feeders but add tidbits of fruits, nut-meats, raisins and baked goods. Migrants are fickle. They may or

*May: Wood ducks nest in May. Ray Sickles, refuge manager at Pennsyl-
vania's Pymatuning Marsh, checks a wood duck box containing 12 eggs.*

may not eat any of this, but if they once find your food and like it, the parade will be endless. You will see orioles, tanagers, warblers, thrushes, flycatchers and vireos. There will be days in May when the trees and shrubs are literally covered with tiny birds eating the insects attracted to the tree blossoms. These are the days when you'll need a pair of binoculars handy to make positive identifications. The birds will all be in breeding plumage, and there should be no problem in recognizing them.

Your birdhouses have been up since April and the first occupants will be looking them over and probably moving in. The male house wren will be busy filling all the available houses with sticks, awaiting the arrival of the female, who will decide for herself which one she will occupy.

Robins will be carrying mud and grass to your shelters or wherever they have decided to nest. They may be fighting their reflections in the cellar or garage windows, too. They think they are fighting a competitive bird of the same species in the glass and are trying to eject it from their newly established territory.

This is the month to finish the planned yard work, new plantings, and the landscaping you dreamed about in January.

By late May, the yard will be alive with activity. Some of the birds will be nesting, others still looking, still others en route to more northern climes. The foliage will be developing from light green to full mature deep colors.

Ah, May! Why can't it be May all year long?

May Checklist:

> Reduce seed feeders, add fruit, nutmeats and raisins for newcomers
> Keep up the suet feeder
> Sugar water feeders should be provided for hummingbirds
> Your water area will be busy. Keep it fresh
> First house occupants will move in
> Replenish nesting material
> Finish plantings and landscaping for summer

JUNE

June is the month to enjoy. The backyard is in full bloom now, not only with flowers, but with all life. The air is filled with songs and the bird world is at its zenith. You have worked hard to bring it to your doorstep, so enjoy the beauty. Sit on the patio and watch the birds bring their youngsters to the feeders for the first time. Watch the robin incubate its four eggs. Peek into the wren house to see if the eggs have hatched.

The feeding station will be at its lowest ebb in June. Maintain the suet feeder, one Niger seed feeder and one sunflower seed feeder. Because the goldfinches nest later than most species, they will still be busy eating Niger seed. Now that the weather is warmer, sit on the patio and enjoy the goldfinches from only a few feet away. It is a great opportunity for photographs.

If your orioles like the fruit, keep putting it out. The migrants are on their home grounds now and the frenzied waves flying north have ended by June. The rest of the summer in your yard will be a maintenance program for the local summer residents and their youngsters.

The water area takes on a new role. Summer residents will need it for drinking and bathing, but their young will find the water the most fascinating spot in your yard. Like the young of all living

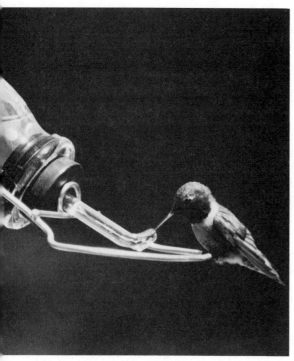

June: A good time to attract hummingbirds to sugar water. This black-chinned hummingbird sips at the sweet liquid at Mile Hi Ranch in Ramsey Canyon, Arizona.

creatures (including human), bird babies will enjoy getting wet for the sake of getting wet. Young robins, in particular, like to wade around in our pool. We have counted nine at one time.

Evening and night birds are very active in June. Listen for whip-poorwills, nighthawks and owls. Spring peepers, American toads and bullfrogs will be calling in nearby ponds and marshes in June.

June Checklist:

Reduce feeders to one each of suet, Niger and sunflower
Feed fruit, nutmeats and raisins if locals like them
Keep water area filled—it will be entertainment for young birds
Hummingbirds should be active at sugar water and blossoms
Migrants are on home territory—everyone is nesting
Listen to the night birds
Enjoy the pinnacle of backyard birding—the nesting and rearing
of young

JULY

The yard will take on a quieter, slower pace in July. The breeding season has peaked and the birds are winding down their domestic chores. There are young birds everywhere: chickadees, downy woodpeckers, robins, cardinals. This is the month when they will teach their progeny that your feeders and water areas are good places to visit.

Maintain one suet, one Niger seed and one sunflower seed feeder through the month of July. There will be less activity at all feeders because the natural food is now so abundant that there is no need to use feeders except out of habit. If the fruit, nutmeats and raisins are popular, keep them up.

The water area will be busy with local catbirds, robins, rose-breasted grosbeaks and various warblers, vireos and tanagers. This is the month when bathing is a welcome respite on a hot day.

Hummingbirds will buzz around your flowers and sugar water feeders. They, too, will have young to bring in for a first visit.

Some of the birdhouses will be filled for a second brood of wrens, chickadees and titmice. The first broods will be flitting around the lawn and shrubs or high in the willow trees. Late July will bring the

July: Water areas are popular during hot summer days. Robins particularly like to cool off with frequent dips.

first signs of a waning summer as some species begin to flock. Blackbirds are particularly visible as they gather in larger and larger groups.

At last, the goldfinches are starting to nest and the pair that has staked out your yard may be having a hard time keeping the others away from the Niger seed feeder. We sometimes take the feeder down for a month, if the fighting gets too fierce.

This is the month to look at your yard. Does it satisfy you? Does it look like the yard you visualized in January? If not, make notes on what you want to do next year. Is there enough cover, food-producing shrubs and nesting sites for birds and other kinds of wild-life? July is the time to evaluate all this for the coming years.

July Checklist:
   Maintain only one suet, Niger seed and sunflower seed feeder each.
   Remove Niger if the nesting goldfinches are fighting
   Water area is loaded with local birds and babies
   The breeding season is winding down—a new sense of content-ment sets in
   Yard is at its peak. Evaluate its functions and appearance

AUGUST

The quiet month for the backyard bird watcher is August. The breeding season for most birds is over. The summer residents are still around but they are less conspicuous. It is too early for migrants, so the backyard is in a quiet holding pattern.

Because of the abundance of natural food, you need maintain only one each of the suet, Niger seed and sunflower seed feeders. They will be used less frequently, but they will have their highlights as roving families visit for the first time.

Water is very important in August. Usually a dry and hot month, August is the peak time for bird bathing. On a 90-degree day, the line-up for the pool will be fascinating. This is the month that some newcomers will slip in for a quick bath. There will be some birds

August: Fruit is popular summer food at the feeding station. This female cardinal enjoys a mixture of bananas, apples and berries contained in a grapefruit half.

there that do not normally frequent bird baths, but because of the weather, they will now.

The fruit and seed-bearing plants in your yard will be popular. Cedar waxwings, robins, orioles and tanagers will flock to the cherry, crab apple and grape.

It is during August that birds begin to lose their breeding plumage. Some waterfowl will become flightless as they molt and grow their winter feathers. Warblers will pass into what we call their "confusing fall plumage," and it will be difficult to differentiate certain species.

Late August is a good time to take down the birdhouses and shelters for the year. Be sure to clean them thoroughly before storing them. Lice and other pests are likely to have remained in the old nests.

In late August, birds are flocking. Swallows, blackbirds and warblers join into larger groups in preparation for the big move south.

August is one of those welcome breaks in the hectic pace of life for birds and humans. It is a time to relax before it all starts again.

August Checklist:

> A quiet month at the feeders. Maintain one each of the suet, Niger seed and sunflower seed feeders
> Notice the popularity of your fruit and seed-bearing plants
> Hot weather makes water essential for attracting birds
> Take down and clean out birdhouses and shelters
> Watch for birds flocking
> Notice the changes of plumages
> Bone up on the identifications of confusing fall warblers

SEPTEMBER

The summer is drawing to an end. Something is happening to the birds in the backyard. The old summer residents are disappearing and there are some new species coming through. The migration south has begun. The warblers, garbed in their "confusing fall plumages," are again in the trees, at the water, in the shrubs. They are moving quickly, as if they have an appointment to keep. They do.

The immature birds have lost their baby looks. They have survived their first summer and join the adults for the flight south.

September: The time to build brush piles for wintering ground birds. Tree and shrub trimmings attract a variety of birds and other wildlife.

The backyard bird watcher needs to think "winter" in September. It is time to create those winter brush piles from fall clippings. Take down the birdhouses if you have not already done so. The martin house is a particularly big job to clean and store.

As in the spring, the water area is attractive to migrants. Bringing them in to the water will allow a closer look and perhaps a better guess at the identity of warblers. September can be hot, and water is always important to birds on hot days.

It is time to put some of the feeders in place. Double the number, if you can, including suet, Niger seed and sunflower seed. Add the wild bird seed mixture to at least one feeder for variety. Put some on the ground, too.

Late September may bring the first junco, though at our feeders it is usually early October.

Yes, September is a new beginning for the backyard bird watcher. It is a time to look forward to snowy days filled with hungry birds at the feeders.

September Checklist:

Double the number of feeders, including suet, Niger, sunflower and wild bird seed mixture

Take down the last of the birdhouses; clean and store

Build up the brush piles from fall cuttings

Watch for the waves of fall migrants, all headed south

Water is important to migrating birds

First junco will arrive in late September or early October

Waterfowl on the move—geese honking in a bright blue or star-studded sky

Summer residents have disappeared; winter is coming

OCTOBER

October is April in reverse. It starts out as one season and ends up as the opposite. Wildlife, particularly bird life, is in a hurry in October. The last of the migrants are rushing through. They may stop long enough for a bath and a drink, or a taste of your offerings at the feeders, but they have important business farther south to attend to.

The first juncos arrive in October. The sight of the "snowbird" carries the message that winter isn't far behind.

Take a look at the goldfinches. The male goldfinch, our favorite indicator of the seasons, has lost his bright yellow plumage by late October.

If you plan to winter over some of the hummingbird flowers, it is time to take them indoors before the first frost gets them.

Chipmunks and gray and red squirrels, if you tolerate them, are all gorging themselves as if it will snow tomorrow. The chipmunk has but a few weeks left to store its winter cache.

The water area is important as always, but watch out for those first freezing days, when the ice may crack the sides of your pool. Now is the time to consider a heater. There are bird bath heaters available from lawn and garden centers and stock tank heaters from farm supply houses if you need something larger. Remember that

October: Canada geese flying south is one of nature's signals that winter is coming.

open, running or dripping water is one of the best ways to get migrating birds to stop in your yard.

Fall trimmings from trees and shrubs make excellent brush piles for wintering ground birds. Juncos, sparrows and many other species seek brush piles for roosting as winter storms approach.

If you haven't increased the number of feeders by now, do so in October. The feeding station will become more and more popular as October days pass. Feed suet, Niger seed, sunflower seed and the wild bird seed mixture in a variety of feeders at the four different levels described in chapter 3.

October is still a good month for waterfowl on lakes. We see families of mallards, teal and scaup. There were canvasbacks and ringnecks on our lake last fall. If we are really lucky, the loon will come through, but in October it is in fall plumage and looks so unlike the black-headed bird we enjoyed in April.

By late October, the transition from summer to winter will be complete. The bird world will have finished its "changing of the guard" as the winter residents settle into your backyard.

October Checklist:

Increase the number of feeders to full winter operation

Feed suet, Niger, sunflower and wild bird seed mixture at the four levels described in chapter 3

Be careful that the water doesn't freeze and crack the pool. Consider the use of a heater to keep the pool open all winter

Build up those brush piles for winter roosting

Record the date of the first junco

Notice the waterfowl, the geese honking overhead

Male goldfinches change from yellow to olive

Squirrels and chipmunks are storing food for winter

The last waves of migrants will pass through heading south

NOVEMBER

This is a time when winter takes over the backyard and the last hold on the carefree days of summer is lost. The summer birds are gone and the winter actors are back on the stage again. Look for tree sparrows, the first evening grosbeaks, the first pine siskins, the first snow.

November: Winter residents have arrived at the feeding station. These goldfinches share the Niger seed feeder with a redpoll on the bottom.

Your winter feeding station should be in full swing now, utilizing all the feeders and the various kinds of foods birds enjoy. Keep in mind that the Niger and sunflower seeds are selective seeds and by using them only, you can exercise some control over the kinds of birds that spend their winter days in your yard.

If you have a heater for keeping the bird bath from freezing, you will find that the birds will respond by using it daily.

The chipmunks will disappear for the year in November, but the gray squirrels will be even more active than ever. Controlling them may be a big problem. Look for help in chapter 6.

Our lake freezes over by late November or very early December. But even in this month of early winter, promises of spring are already there for those who look hard at tree buds and the myriad seeds that will grow next summer's green bonanza.

November Checklist:

Feeding station in full swing. Use a variety of seeds, suet and bird cakes to attract the maximum number of species

Exert control, if desired, by selective feeding with Niger and sunflower seeds

Water heaters will keep the pool from freezing and the birds happy

Notice that the chipmunks are gone, but the gray squirrels are voracious

The winter residents have arrived, including tree sparrows, whitethroats and juncos

Winter grips the land, but buds and seeds speak of spring to come

DECEMBER

North or South, winter is upon the land. It is the time when the heaviest bird feeder use begins. Put the last of the feeders up and fill them with a variety of seeds, including Niger, sunflower and wild bird seed mixture. Be sure to cover the four feeding niches discussed in chapter 3.

Suet is also important as an energy food and to keep the woodpeckers happy. Make bird cakes for those species you want to spoil.

The first really big snowstorms will hit the backyard and feeders should be brushed clear of snow so that birds can eat. If the birds

December: Many backyard bird watchers like to decorate Christmas trees for birds.

are feeding in a frenzy before a storm hits, perhaps filling the feeders again at midday will help them better prepare for several days of cold, windy weather.

This is the month that the Canadian invaders could arrive, if they come at all. Look for evening grosbeaks, pine siskins, redpolls and crossbills in addition to the regulars, which will include chickadees, titmice, juncos, tree, white-throated, white-crowned and song sparrows, cardinals, nuthatches, goldfinches, purple finches and woodpeckers. This kind of action should keep everyone fascinated.

Open water on subfreezing days will delight many of the birds and they will reward you with frequent visits.

Some people like to decorate a "Birds' Christmas Tree" during the holiday season. Read chapter 3 for details on what to use and how to decorate. These backyard bird watchers believe that the yellow-, red- and blue-feathered ornaments on the birds' Christmas tree are the season's brightest decorations.

And don't discard your indoor Christmas tree in January. Plan to tie it to a fence post or another tree to give a little more cover in your yard for months, sometimes years to come.

December Checklist:

Fill feeders daily. A variety of food in widely placed feeders brings the greatest number of birds to backyards

Exercise control by using only Niger, sunflower and suet

Open water on a subfreezing day is irresistible to many birds

Watch for an invasion of evening and pine grosbeaks, pine siskins, redpolls and crossbills

Decorate a Birds' Christmas Tree for the prettiest tree of all

Don't discard that indoor tree—convert it to outside cover

Organizations of Interest
to Birders

American Birding Association
P.O. Box 4335
Austin, Texas 78765
PUBLICATION:
  Birding

American Ornithologists' Union,
  Inc.
National Museum of Natural
  History
Smithsonian Institution
Washington, D.C. 20560
PUBLICATIONS:
  The Auk
  Ornithological Monographs

Bird Populations Institute
Kansas State University
P.O. Box 637
Manhattan, Kansas 66502
PUBLICATION:
  The Bird Watch

Brooks Bird Club
707 Warwood Avenue
Wheeling, West Virginia 26003
PUBLICATIONS:
  The Redstart
  The Mailbag

Canadian Nature Federation
46 Elgin Street
Ottawa, Ontario K1P 5K6
PUBLICATION:
  Nature Canada

Canadian Wildlife Federation
1673 Carling Avenue
Ottawa, Ontario K2A 1C4
PUBLICATIONS:
  Wildlife Report
  International Wildlife
  Ottawa Report
  Pipeline Update

Cooper Ornithological Society
% Stephen M. Russell
Department of Ecology and
  Evolutionary Biology
University of Arizona
Tucson, Arizona 85721
PUBLICATIONS:
  The Condor
  Pacific Coast Avifauna

Cornell Laboratory of Ornithology
159 Sapsucker Woods Road
Ithaca, New York 14850
PUBLICATIONS:
  The Living Bird
  Members' Newsletter

Hawk Mountain Sanctuary
  Association
R.D. 2
Kempton, Pennsylvania 19529
PUBLICATION:
  Members' Newsletter

Massachusetts Audubon Society,
  Inc.
South Great Road
Lincoln, Massachusetts 01773
PUBLICATIONS:
  Newsletter
  Man & Nature (yearbook)
  Curious Naturalist

National Audubon Society
950 Third Avenue
New York, New York 10022
PUBLICATIONS:
  Audubon
  Audubon Leader
  American Birds

National Wildlife Federation
1412 Sixteenth Street N.W.
Washington, D.C. 20036
PUBLICATIONS:
  National Wildlife
  International Wildlife
  Ranger Rick's Nature Magazine

Wilson Ornithological Society
% Jerome A. Jackson
Department of Zoology
Mississippi State University
Mississippi State, Mississippi
  39762
PUBLICATION:
  The Wilson Bulletin

Some Manufacturers of Bird Feeders, Birdhouses and Bird Bath Equipment

Ardsley Woodcraft Products, Inc.
263 Douglas Road
Staten Island, New York 10304
  Bird feeders and food

Barzen of Minneapolis, Inc.
P.O. Box 1123
Minneapolis, Minnesota 55440
  Bird feeders and houses

Ben Smith Martin Houses
Bailey's Habor, Wisconsin 40202
  Birdhouses, especially martin houses

Beverly Specialties Company
Box 9
Riverside, Illinois 60546
  Sprays for bird baths

Droll Yankees, Inc.
Mill Road
Foster, Rhode Island 02825
  Bird feeders

Duncraft
25 South Main Street
Penacook, New Hampshire 03301
  Bird feeders, food and houses

Garden Galleries
150 Lyceum Street
Geneva, New York 14456
  Birdhouses, suet cake feeders

Heath Manufacturing Company
140 Mill Street
Coopersville, Michigan 49404
  Bird feeders, baths and birdhouses

Hummingbird Heaven
6618-A Apperson Street
Tujunga, California 91042
  Feeders for hummingbirds, orioles and tanagers

Hyde Bird Feeder Company
56 Felton Street
Waltham, Massachusetts 02154
  A complete line of birdhouses, bird feeders and bird cakes

Little Giant Pump Company
2810 North Tulsa Street
Oklahoma City, Oklahoma 73112
   Pumps for recirculating ponds
   and waterfalls

Massachusetts Audubon Society
155 Newbury Street
Boston, Massachusetts 02116
   Complete line of birdhouses,
   feeders and food

North Star Industries
3650 Fremont Avenue North
Minneapolis, Minnesota 55412
   Kits for bird feeders and houses

Smith-Gates Corporation
Farmington, Connecticut 06032
   Heaters for bird baths

Welles L. Bishop
1245 East Main Street
Meriden, Connecticut 06452
   Birdhouses and feeders

Woodland Specialties
Box 395
Hempstead, New York 11951
   Bird feeders

Yield House
North Conway
New Hampshire 03860
   Kits for martin houses

Other Books of Interest to the Backyard Bird Watcher

Arbib, Robert, and Tony Soper. *The Hungry Bird Book.* New York: Taplinger Publishing Company, 1971.

Austin, E.S., and O.L. Austin, Jr. *The Random House Book of Birds.* New York: Random House, 1970.

Barrington, Rupert. *A Garden for Your Birds.* New York: Grosset & Dunlap, 1971.

Bent, Arthur Cleveland. *Life Histories of North American Birds.* 23 volumes. New York: Dover Publications, 1962–64.

Bull, John, and John Farrand, Jr. *The Audubon Society Field Guide to North American Birds. Eastern Region.* New York: Alfred A. Knopf, 1977.

Dennis, John V. *A Complete Guide to Bird Feeding.* New York: Alfred A. Knopf, 1975.

Gillam, Harry L. *More Wildlife on Your Property.* Richmond: Virginia Commission of Game and Inland Fisheries, 1973.

Godfrey, W. E. *The Birds of Canada.* Montreal: National Museum of Canada, 1966.

Griffin, D. R. *Bird Migration.* New York: Dover Publications, 1974.

Harrison, Hal H. *A Field Guide to Birds' Nests in the Eastern U.S.* Boston: Houghton Mifflin, 1975.

Harrison, Hal H. *A Field Guide to Birds' Nests in the Western U.S.* Boston: Houghton Mifflin, 1979.

Hickey, Joseph J. *A Guide to Bird Watching.* New York: Dover Publications, 1975.

Hines, Robert. *Fifty Birds of Town and City.* Washington, D.C.: U.S. Government Printing Office, 1973.

277

Lawrence, L. de K. *The Lovely and the Wild*. New York: McGraw-Hill, 1969.

Laycock, George. *The Birdwatcher's Bible*. Garden City, N.Y.: Doubleday & Co., Inc., 1976.

Mason, C. Russell. *Picture Primer of Attracting Birds*. Boston: Houghton Mifflin, 1952.

McElroy, T. P., Jr. *The Habitat Guide to Birding*. New York: Alfred A. Knopf, 1974.

National Wildlife Federation, *Gardening with Wildlife*. Washington, D.C.: National Wildlife Federation, 1974.

Peterson, Roger Tory. *A Field Guide to the Birds*. Boston: Houghton Mifflin, 1947.

Peterson, Roger Tory. *A Field Guide to Western Birds*. Boston: Houghton Mifflin, 1961.

Peterson, Roger Tory. *How to Know the Birds*. Boston: Houghton Mifflin, 1949.

Reilly, E. M., Jr. *The Illustrated Handbook of North American Birds*. New York: McGraw-Hill, 1968.

Robbins, Chandler S., Bertel Bruun, Herbert S. Zim and Arthur Singer. *Birds of North America*. New York: Golden Press, 1966.

Sawyer, Edmund J. *Homes for Wildlife—Baths and Feeding Shelters*. Bloomfield Hills, Mich.: Cranbrook Institute of Science, 1969.

Schutz, Walter E. *Bird Watching, Housing and Feeding*. Milwaukee: Bruce Publishing Company, 1963.

Skutch, Alexander F. *The Life of the Hummingbird*. New York: Crown Publishers, 1973.

Sparks, J. *Bird Behavior*. New York: Grosset and Dunlap, 1970.

Stefferud, A., and A. L. Nelson, eds. *Birds in Our Lives*. Washington, D.C.: U.S. Government Printing Office, 1966.

Terres, John K. *How Birds Fly: Under the Water and Through the Air*. New York: Hawthorn Books, 1975.

Terres, John K. *Songbirds in Your Garden*. New York: Hawthorn Books, 1977.

Udvardy, Miklos D. F. *The Audubon Society Field Guide to North American Birds. Western Region*. New York: Alfred A. Knopf, 1977.

Wetmore, Alexander. *Song and Garden Birds of North America*. Washington, D.C.: National Geographic Society, 1964.

Other Items of Interest to the Backyard Bird Watcher

HOME STUDY COURSE IN ORNITHOLOGY

For information, write to:
  Seminars in Ornithology
  Laboratory of Ornithology
  Cornell University
  159 Sapsucker Woods Road
  Ithaca, New York 14850

RECORDINGS OF BIRD SONGS

Several are available from the Cornell Laboratory of Ornithology, including one which follows the Peterson *Field Guide to the Birds* (both East and West). For a complete listing and prices, write to:
  Laboratory of Ornithology
  Cornell University
  159 Sapsucker Woods Road
  Ithaca, New York 14850

Index

[*Italic* page numbers indicate illustrations.]

ABOUT THE AUTHOR

George H. Harrison is a writer, photographer and consultant in the field of natural history and the outdoors. For nine years he was managing editor of *National* and *International Wildlife* magazines and has been the field editor since 1974. Currently, Mr. Harrison is nature editor for *Sports Afield.*

President of Harrison Productions, Inc., of Hubertus, Wisconsin, Mr. Harrison is also consultant to the Bushnell Division of Bausch & Lomb, and to the Darby Drug Company of Rockville Centre, New York, for their "Wildlife Heritage Cards."

George and his wife—and frequent coauthor—Kit, lead an annual safari to East Africa. World travelers, they have visited more than forty-five countries on five continents in search of wildlife stories and photographs. They live in Wisconsin.